VISUAL SCIENCE
ENERGY

Desmond Boyle

Silver Burdett Company

Editor John Rowlstone
Design Richard Garratt
Consultant Tony Osman
Picture Research Jenny Golden
Production John Moulder

First published 1980

Macdonald Educational Ltd
Holywell House
Worship Street
London EC2A 2EN

© Macdonald Educational 1980

Adapted and Published in
the United States by
Silver Burdett Company,
Morristown, New Jersey

1982 Printing

ISBN 0-382-06658-8

Library of Congress
Catalog Card No. 82-50390

Cover: oil refinery in Peru
Right: several forms and sources
of energy

Contents

What is energy?

Above: Most of our light energy comes from the Sun. Even though light travels at 300,000 kilometres a second, the light from these stars has taken many years to reach the Earth.

Above: The candle and match are sources of heat and light energy. The head of the match is impregnated with chemicals, and these store energy. The chemical energy is released by striking the match.

Above: Lightning is a spectacular display of nature's electrical energy. It originates in thunderclouds when the positive and negative electric charges in water droplets separate out in the freezing process.

The steam train shows many energy forms. The mechanical energy that drives the wheels of the locomotive is supplied by the heat of the steam which is in turn provided by the chemical energy of coal.

Energy can be defined as the capacity to do work. Matter and energy form the basis of everything in life. Matter is more 'solid' and tangible than energy. Energy influences matter by heating, moving or 'electrifying' it.

Energy is also always associated with change. Physical, chemical or biological changes take place when energy is converted from one form into another, for example when the chemical energy of fuels is converted into heat energy. During these changes the total amount of energy available is unaltered. Energy cannot be created or destroyed.

Forms of energy

This total amount of energy is scattered throughout the universe in a great variety of different forms. These include such familiar concepts as heat, light, electrical and sound energy. Although other concepts used may not be so well known, the energy forms which they represent should be easily recognizable.

'Potential' is a general word used to describe any kind of stored energy. The firing of a simple catapult could be described as 'an investigation of the potential energy of a stretched elastic band'. The potential energy of an atomic bomb is capable of causing a vast amount of destruction, while a nuclear power station harnesses the same potential energy for man's use. Potential energy can be found in the chemical potential energy of the calculator battery or in the gravitational potential energy of the waters trapped behind a hydro-electric power dam.

Kinetic energy is the energy an object possesses because it is moving. From the invisible electron orbiting an atomic nucleus to a large star in its path across the universe, all moving objects possess kinetic energy in proportion to both their mass and their speed.

Other forms include the mechanical energy that is used in digging a garden, and the radiant energy that arrives as sunlight in the form of both heat and light. The energy needed by living cells is provided by the chemical energy released from food being processed by the body.

All energy forms can be roughly divided into two types – high and low grade. Electrical energy is described as high grade because it can conveniently be converted into other useful forms. To change low temperature heat into any other kind of energy is difficult. For this reason heat is usually described as low grade energy.

Above: Sound energy can produce sensations of quiet pleasure or deafening pain. Aeroplanes travelling faster than the speed of sound send out shock waves known as sonic booms.

Above: Gravity causes water above sea-level to flow downwards towards the sea. The water has a gravitational potential energy which is converted into kinetic energy as it flows.

Potential energy is stored in both the stretched bowstring and the bow itself. When the tight bowstring is released, the arrow gains the kinetic energy of all moving objects.

Above: The energy released by a nuclear bomb destroys everything in its path. Nuclear reactors control the nuclear reaction and convert it into useful electricity.

Below: This meter measures the units of electrical energy used in your home and enables the electricity bill to be worked out.

Units of measurement

There are as many different units for measuring energy as there are energy forms. To avoid confusion scientists have adopted an international system (SI) of units. In this system only one unit is used to measure all energy forms. It is called the joule (J) after the 19-century scientist James Prescott Joule, who measured the heat produced by mechanical energy.

The joule is quite a small unit of energy. A 100-watt household light bulb uses 100J of electrical energy every second it is on. Most electricity suppliers measure electrical energy in a non-SI unit, the kilowatt hour. This is equivalent to 3,600,000 joules. But the kilowatt hour is a very small unit when it comes to measuring the energy consumption of a nation. A larger unit now in use is the mtce (million tonnes of coal equivalent). This is the energy available from one million tonnes of coal and is equal to approximately 10,000 million kilowatt hours. In 1978 the total energy consumption of the United Kingdom from coal, oil, natural gas, nuclear, hydro-electric and other sources was 339.8 mtce.

Power

Power is the rate of doing work and its SI unit is the watt. This represents an energy consumption of one joule every second. An average power station might generate about 500 megawatts (MW). This means that it produces 500 million joules of energy every second. The terms energy and power are often interchanged in the mistaken belief that they mean the same thing.

Electricity meter

Energy sources

Most of our energy comes from the Sun in one way or other. The Sun's energy enables plants to make the food which animals and man eat. The Sun's energy is stored in the coal, wood and oil which man burns to do work for him. Man's development is itself closely tied to his discovery of new energy sources.

Elements

The natural energy sources of the Sun, wind and water satisfy only a small part of man's total energy needs. The Sun distributes its heat and light energy unevenly over the surface of the Earth. Equatorial regions receive more than enough heat whilst permanent ice caps in the polar regions are a result of too little heat. For centuries the wind has enabled sailing ships to sail the seas or man to pump up water or grind grain. Watermills were used to convert the kinetic energy of fast-flowing streams into useful mechanical energy.

Today, great interest is being shown in the development of alternative and more efficient ways of using the natural energy sources available. These energy sources are very important because they can be regarded as renewable, i.e. man expects to be able to call upon them for as long as there is life on Earth.

If the winds were harnessed then windmills could become an important source of electrical power. In the future geothermal energy, using heat from the Earth's interior, may become an important energy source for many countries as this too may be considered renewable. The tides and the waves are both energy sources with great potential. The latter awaits a breakthrough in engineering technology before it can be considered commercially viable.

Fuels

A fuel is a source of potential energy which can be readily converted into heat. The ideal fuel should also be safe, cheap and non-polluting. From marsh gas to camel dung, man has always been inventive in his choice of fuels. But no fuel yet developed passes the above conditions. Today, coal, oil and natural

ELEMENTS

Sun

Wind

Water

Earth

gas are the important, but far from ideal, fuels. The point about these natural fuels, whether solid, liquid or gas, is that they are non-renewable. Once they are used up there are no further supplies to draw upon.

Nuclear energy is the latest and potentially most dangerous fuel that man has identified. It harnesses the

Below: Nature's elements of Sun, wind, water and the Earth provide us with an inexhaustible store of energy. But often this energy can be difficult to capture and control. Fuels are much more convenient to use but world supplies are running out. In the future we will have to rely much more on the elements to satisfy our energy needs.

energy from the nucleus of the atom and the forces that hold this matter together.

Another type of fuel is provided by the carbohydrate glucose. It acts as an energy source for our cells and is perhaps the only fuel without which man could not survive for long.

The energy crisis
The total energy output from the Sun that falls on the surface of the Earth, although in the form of low-grade heat, is more than enough to satisfy all man's energy needs. Unfortunately, this energy mainly goes to waste as man has yet to develop an efficient way to capture this energy for work. Only green

plants use it on a large scale.

The energy crisis represents a growing awareness of man's limited resources for producing high-grade energy at a time when our reserves of fuel are rapidly dwindling. Even if it is too big a problem for our present technology to solve yet, there are several ways in which the worst of its effects can be lessened. Firstly, there is the conservation of our valuable and limited resources of energy. Second, the use of both nuclear and biological fuels will become increasingly important for the survival of mankind. Third, a great deal of money will have to be spent on research into more efficient ways of using alternative sources.

FUELS

Coal

Gas

Oil

Plants

Nuclear

Energy from the sun

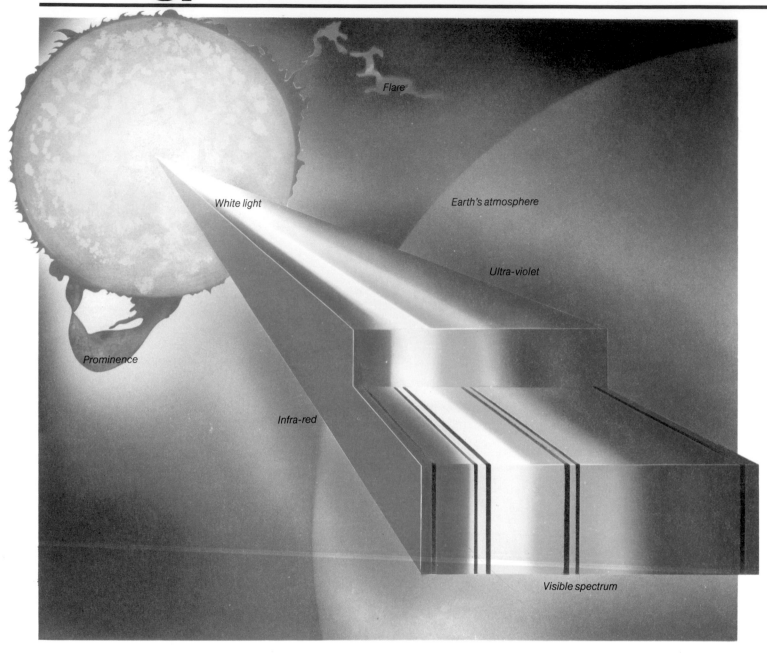

Flare

White light

Earth's atmosphere

Ultra-violet

Prominence

Infra-red

Visible spectrum

The Sun has been radiating vast amounts of energy for at least the past 2,000 million years and will continue to do so for thousands of millions of years to come.

A complex series of nuclear reactions within the Sun is responsible for the release of all this energy. The temperature at its centre is thought to reach 20,000,000°C.

This energy arrives in the Earth's atmosphere in the form of solar radiation. Much of it is direct sunlight while the rest is scattered by the atmosphere to form the more diffuse background light. If just 0.01 per cent of this radiation could be turned into high-grade energy it would be sufficient to satisfy all mankind's present needs.

Solar collectors

Solar collectors are often mounted on south-facing roofs to capture both direct and diffuse solar radiation. For maximum efficiency the sides and back of any collector system must be made of insulating material, while the plate surface should be matt black to absorb as much radiation as possible. The whole system can then be covered with either single or double glass panels.

About 50 per cent of the small amount of energy which the black plate reflects is re-radiated by the covering glass panel back down onto the plate. The re-radiation of this energy by the glass is known as the greenhouse effect. This is effectively how a greenhouse manages to keep its temperature inside

Above: Energy from the Sun travels 150 million kilometres through empty space before reaching the Earth's atmosphere. Only a small part of the Sun's radiation, known as the visible spectrum, can be detected by the human eye. At either side of the visible spectrum lie invisible infra-red and ultra-violet radiation. Both the Sun's and the Earth's atmospheres absorb certain bands of the spectrum so that in fact it is the absorption spectrum of light that filters through to Earth.

Right: People living in this house have a solar-heated water supply. Energy from the sun is used to heat the fluid which flows under the flat plates on the roof. These are black because this colour absorbs heat.

higher than that of the surrounding air.

A liquid, usually water and antifreeze, flows in a closed system beneath the plates. A heat exchanger is used to extract the energy from the heated liquid. It works by transferring heat between fluids without the fluids being in contact with each other.

In temperate climates a few collector plates can work efficiently enough to provide the energy to maintain an adequate domestic hot water system. However, flat plate collectors can only provide heat at temperatures less than 100°C. Where temperatures greater than 100°C are required, it is necessary to use mirrors to focus the Sun's rays. Legend has it that more than 2,000 years ago Archimedes used just such a system to set fire to the Roman fleet that was besieging his native city of Syracuse. Focusing collectors depend on the energy from direct sunlight, and therefore operate effectively only on clear, sunny days. Concave focusing collectors must continually follow the path of the Sun across the sky.

Solar cells

Batteries of solar cells can convert either diffuse or direct sunlight into electrical energy. This process (photo-voltaic conversion) does not depend upon

heat, as experiments with solar cells at the South Pole have recently shown.

Semi-conductors can be used to convert light energy directly into electricity. Cadmium sulphide (CdS) and silicon (Si) are the most common semiconductors. CdS cells are less stable but are cheaper to manufacture. At present solar batteries are too expensive to be considered for use in large-scale power

Above: The power of the Sun's rays here warm the surface waters, encouraging the growth of plankton. Only plants successfully make use of this huge energy source.

stations. Chemical storage batteries are often used alongside solar systems as a kind of insurance policy. The excess energy produced on sunny days is stored for cloudy days with little direct sunlight.

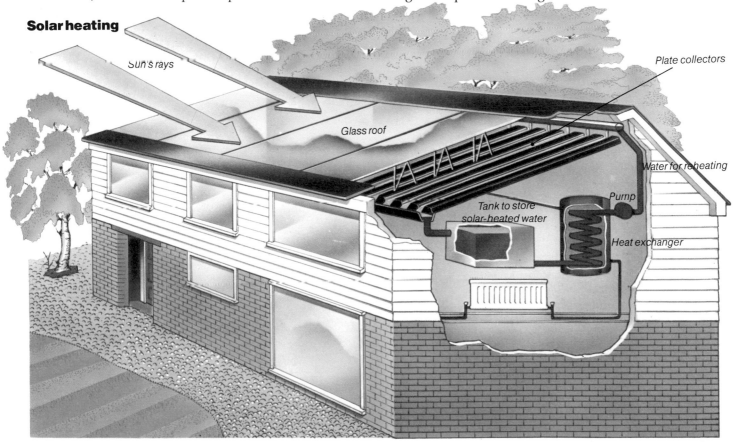

Solar heating

Sun's rays

Plate collectors

Glass roof

Water for reheating

Tank to store solar-heated water

Pump

Heat exchanger

Water power

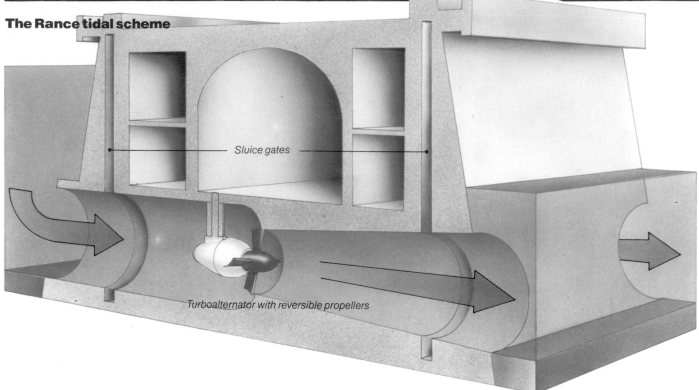

Above: This is a diagram of the Rance estuary tidal power station. Tidal waters flowing in and out of the estuary cause the turboalternators to generate electricity.

Below: The spectacular Kaprun dam lies in the Austrian Hohe Tauern range. At the base of the dam, generators convert the kinetic energy of the fast-flowing water into electricity.

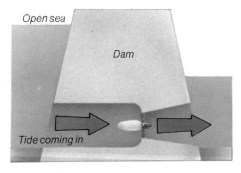

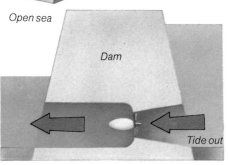

One of the most impressive works of modern engineering is a massive hydro-electric power dam. Where watermills once made use of wheels and cogs to bring about the conversion of the kinetic energy of water flowing downstream into mechanical energy, hydro-electric power plants now use turbines to convert it into electrical energy.

Hydro-electricity

Hydro-electric dams work on the simple principle that the greater the vertical distance between the water reservoir behind the dam and the turbines at the base of the dam, the more power can be generated.

Although hydro-electric energy is both renewable and does not cause air pollution, the use of dams to trap the water may result in the flooding of wide areas of useful land. Most industrialized countries have already built hydro-electric power stations on the more favourable sites. Canada, for example, gets about 75 per cent of its electrical energy from hydro-electric power. Unfortunately, favourable sites often lie in the most inhospitable and inaccessible areas and this adds greatly to the already high capital cost of building these dams.

A very important feature of the stations with high dams is their capacity for energy storage. At off-peak periods, surplus electricity can be used to pump water from lower levels back through the turbines and up to the reservoir. The potential energy thus gained by the water can later be converted into electricity when the demand is high. This is a pumped storage scheme.

Tidal energy

In the 12th century, watermills in Brittany were driven by the flow of tidal waters, and today France still leads the world in the harnessing of tidal energy. With a generating capacity of 240,000 kW from a bank of 24 turbines, the Rance River Project near St Malo is the world's largest tidal power station. The generators are driven by the waters of the tide as it flows both in and out of the Rance estuary twice a day. The level in the estuary varies by as much as 10 metres. The generators also act as pumps to increase the tidal flow into the basin during periods of 'neap' tides. By 'over filling' the reservoir in this way, additional water can be stored and later

released to generate electricity at times of peak demand.

Several other countries are now investigating the possibility of building similar generating stations. The capital cost of constructing such power stations is very great, and the number of suitable sites limited.

Wave power

The amount of power available from waves varies considerably with

Above: This picturesque old watermill is in the Black Forest region of Germany.

changes in the weather, but recent estimates suggest that an average of 50 kW of power could theoretically be extracted from each metre of wavefront. At present the very best device would find difficulty in converting even 15 kW of this energy into useful electricity. A practical power station would have to be several kilometres long, and this would present a hazard to shipping.

Wave power

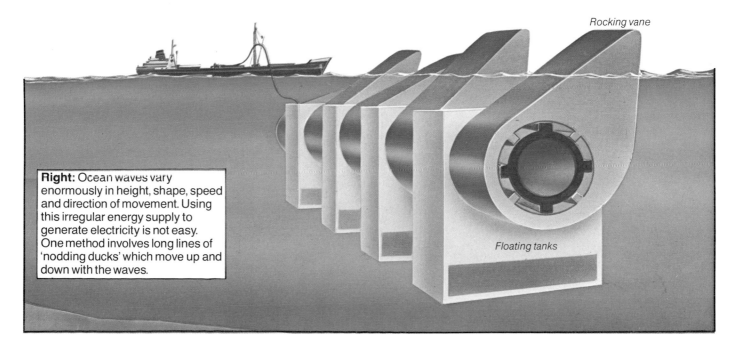

Rocking vane

Right: Ocean waves vary enormously in height, shape, speed and direction of movement. Using this irregular energy supply to generate electricity is not easy. One method involves long lines of 'nodding ducks' which move up and down with the waves.

Floating tanks

Wind power

Fuel shortages may one day create new interest in the commercial use of sailing ships, but the real importance of wind power lies in the development of stationary machines for converting wind energy into electricity. In the past all mechanical devices for extracting energy from the wind were called windmills, but today the word aerogenerator is becoming quite commonly used.

Holland is often thought of as the home of windmills and, indeed, by the end of the 18th century more than 20,000 windmills were in use in the Netherlands. Most of these were used to pump water from low-lying areas and so reclaim useful land from the sea. Nowadays many more countries are benefiting from wind power, and in 1975 it was estimated that 150,000 small windmills were in operation in the USA.

Wind speed

An instrument for measuring wind speed is called an anemometer. The most common type consists of three

small cups mounted on a vertical spindle. The greater the wind speed, the faster the rate of rotation of the cups. Quite accurate estimates of wind speed can also be made by experienced observers without the aid of instruments. Such estimates are usually reported as points on the Beaufort Scale, which ranges from Force 0 (calm) to Force 12 (hurricane).

The power of the wind depends upon the cube of the wind velocity (v^3), and this means that even quite small fluctuations in wind speed will cause large changes in available power. For example, a 20 per cent reduction in wind speed would cut the wind power by almost half. Very light winds are not sufficient to turn most generators, while damage may occur if the machine is operated in winds in excess of 30 metres per second.

Left: Windmills were probably first used for milling grain or lifting water in Persia about the 7th century AD. They became a feature of the European landscape from the 13th century onwards.

Windmill

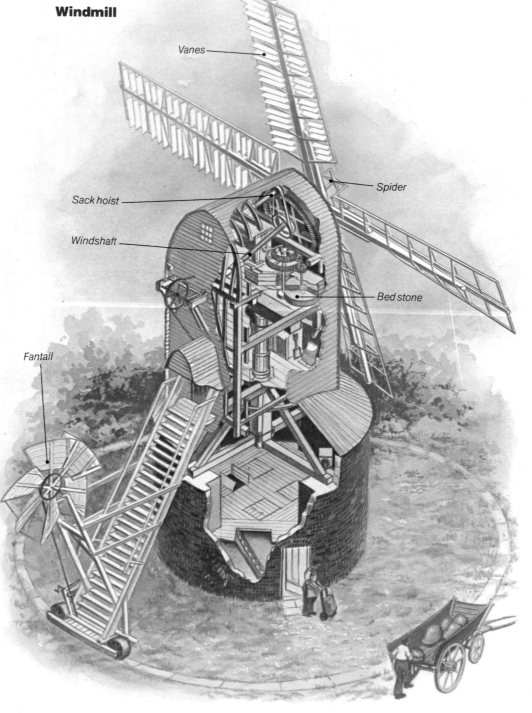

Vanes

Spider

Sack hoist

Windshaft

Bed stone

Fantail

Left: With favourable winds large sailing ships can travel long distances at great speed. The time may well come again when large sailing ships are used for international trade.

13.4 metres per second. This project was abandoned after only 23 days of operation when one of the rotor blades broke.

It is perhaps significant that in 1962, in France, similar damage was sustained by the world's second largest windmill, and this too was never replaced. Although small windmills have been operating successfully for hundreds of years, current experience shows that the engineering problems associated with large-scale structures have still to be overcome before progress can be made.

Future potential

The most suitable sites are either offshore or in mountainous regions. Most countries therefore have great potential for the large-scale development of wind power. The principal obstacles to such projects include development costs, interruptions to the supply because of weather conditions, and problems of transporting electricity from offshore sites to where it is needed.

Aerogenerator designs

There are two distinct types of aerogenerators – vertical axis and horizontal axis machines. Vertical axis generators turn like spinning tops in the wind and are therefore operated by winds from any direction. However, they are not very efficient and therefore are not so widely used as the more conventional type. Traditional horizontal axis machines can have any number of blades, but recent work has shown that designs with two blades are the most efficient.

The larger the diameter of the rotor blades then the greater is the available energy. The most powerful aerogenerator ever built was constructed during World War II in Vermont, USA. With two rotor blades, 53 metres in diameter, the machine was designed to produce 1.25 MW at a wind speed of

Right: This house combines the power of the wind as generated by a two-blade wind turbine with solar panels to provide heating and light. Very high winds can cause turbine blades to break.

Heat from the Earth

The spectacular release of energy from an erupting volcano provides dramatic proof of the great store of energy which lies beneath our feet.

Underground geology

On average, between 30 and 40 kilometres of solid rock separates us from a layer of hot molten rock called magma. This layer is thought to be some 2,900 kilometres thick. The magma is too deep, too hot, and too dangerously unpredictable to be used directly as an energy source. However, some of its heat escapes slowly outwards towards the upper layer of rocks which constitute the Earth's crust. Occasionally, unusual geological formations cause water to be trapped in porous rocks a few kilometres below the surface of the Earth. The trapped water then slowly absorbs much of the outward flowing heat to produce a vast reservoir of hot geothermal fluids. Geysers and hot springs are formed where natural cracks in the overlying rocks allow some of these hot fluids to escape to the surface.

Below: This slice out of the Earth shows how the temperature increases dramatically towards the molten core.

Using geothermal energy

The use of geothermal energy for heating dates back at least to the era of the ancient Roman bath house. Several of these have been preserved and restored to working order. Its large-scale exploitation has, however, had to await the arrival of 20th-century technology.

Above: A geothermal power station in El Salvador uses heat from inside the Earth to generate electricity.

Iceland has not been slow to exploit its volcanoes, geysers and hot springs. Geothermal district heating schemes already supply the capital of Reykjavik with all its heating. To prevent wasteful heat losses from the hot water pipes which carry the energy from the generating site is both difficult and expensive. For this reason geothermal district heating is not possible in areas which are far from the geothermal source. The French, too, are fortunate in having many such sources close to centres of population, and hope by 1990 to have 500,000 homes heated by geothermal energy.

Electricity generation

In 1904 at Lardarello in Italy, Prince Piero Conti first connected an electricity generator to a steam engine driven by natural steam and began the age of geothermal electricity.

For the generation of electricity, the hot steam and other geothermal fluids must be at a high enough pressure to operate the turbines. By sinking wells, often thousands of metres into the Earth's crust, it is possible to break into the natural underground reservoirs of

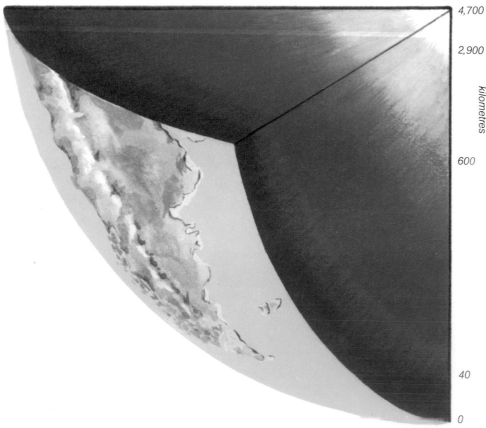

Surface plates 0-1,000°C	Mantle 1,000-2,000°C	Lower mantle 2,000-4,500°C	Core >4,500°C

4,700

2,900

kilometres

600

40

0

Right: Rivers of white-hot molten lava pour down the slopes of Mount Etna from deep inside the Earth. These eruptions are spectacular proof of the Earth's fiery interior.

Right: Geysers are caused by the heating of water deep in the Earth's crust. When steam forms due to the great temperatures and pressures down there, it forces the water up and out via fissures in the Earth's crust.

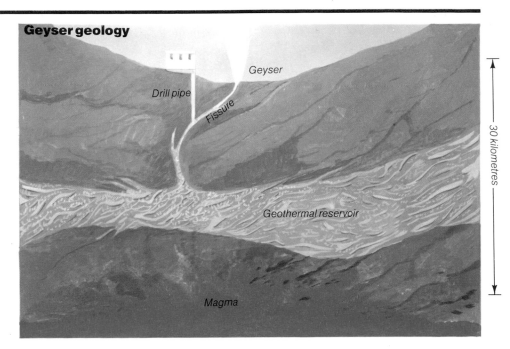

Geyser geology

Geyser

Drill pipe

Fissure

Geothermal reservoir

Magma

30 kilometres

water and steam under high pressure. The steam then rushes to the surface where it is used to power the electricity generators.

Although such power stations may be expensive to set up, once they are established they will provide a stable supply of electricity for very many years to come. Already the USA, New Zealand and Japan have large geothermal power stations feeding electricity to their national grids.

The future

Some countries which do not have underground reservoirs are considering sinking two wells some distance apart into porous rocks underground. By pumping cold water down one well it is hoped to obtain a supply of hot steam from the other by thus cooling the rocks and warming the water.

Since heat flows very slowly outwards from the centre of the Earth, energy extracted from the reservoirs is not immediately replaced. Geothermal energy is therefore not renewable during any one person's lifetime, but will eventually be replaced over a much longer period of time. However, the source of energy is essentially constant.

Energy convertors

Generator

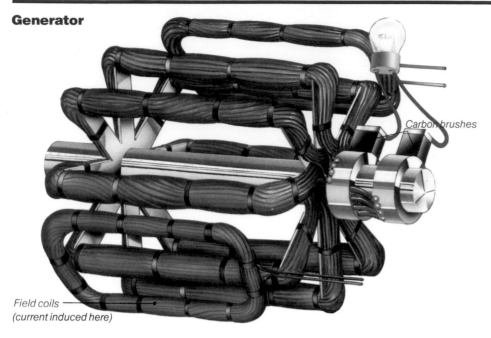

Carbon brushes

Field coils
(current induced here)

Left: This is an electrical generator which converts mechanical energy into electrical energy. When a coil of wire rotates in a magnetic field, electricity is generated. Here the magnetic field comes from the field windings on either side of the coils.

Any form of energy can ultimately be converted into any other. This interchangeability of energy forms is its most important property.

Man continually attempts to reproduce nature's many and varied energy conversions. Plants absorb light to create stores of chemical energy. The plants are later eaten by animals. The long chain of energy changes which begins with this simple action, is in essence, the process of life itself.

By using either one convertor, or a whole series of convertors, it is possible to carry out almost any desired energy conversion. A hydro-electric power station, for example, uses the following system to produce electricity. The gravitational potential of trapped water is first converted into the kinetic energy of moving water. The dam's turbines then convert this into mechanical energy and the generators convert the mechanical energy into electricity.

Efficiency

The percentage of input energy which is finally changed into useful output is known as the efficiency of the convertor. An 80 per cent efficient dynamo would therefore change only 80 joules out of every 100 joules of input energy into electricity. Most of the remaining 20 joules end up as heat, although sound and mechanical energy may also be produced. In practice this kind of efficiency would be marvellous. Since some form of unwanted energy is always produced in convertors, no system is ever 100 per cent efficient.

Any reduction in the amount of unwanted energy produced by a convertor automatically results in an improvement in efficiency. The downhill skier who carefully waxes his skis and crouches low whilst in motion is striving to ensure that a large percentage of his potential energy is converted into kinetic energy. A fluorescent light is three times more efficient than a filament lamp because it produces much less heat energy. It glows by converting electrical energy directly into visible light without using the hot wire filament of a conventional light bulb.

Waste heat recovery systems can be used where energy convertors inevitably produce large amounts of heat. A few large power stations now use the heat produced by their generators to provide district heating for neighbouring buildings.

Escalator

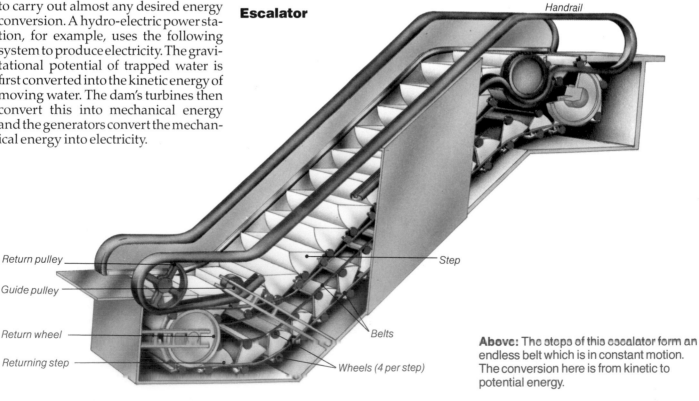

Handrail

Return pulley

Guide pulley

Return wheel

Returning step

Step

Belts

Wheels (4 per step)

Above: The steps of this escalator form an endless belt which is in constant motion. The conversion here is from kinetic to potential energy.

Four-stroke engine

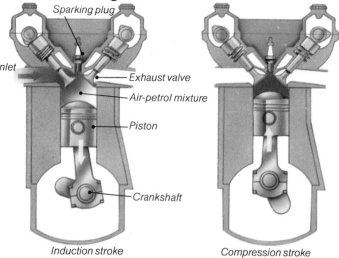

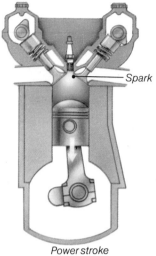

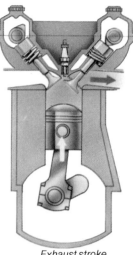

Sparking plug

Inlet

Exhaust valve

Air-petrol mixture

Piston

Crankshaft

Spark

Induction stroke   *Compression stroke*   *Power stroke*   *Exhaust stroke*

Below: A battery is one of the few devices capable of storing electrical energy. Chemical reactions between the lead plates and the sulphuric acid store the energy needed to drive an electrical current round a circuit.

Battery

Negative terminal

Positive terminal

Electrical connector

Cell divider

Lead plates

Vacuum cleaner

Dust bag

Inlet tube

Fans

Electric motor

Suction pump

Friction

Friction is a force which acts between two surfaces which are in contact and opposes their motion. Air friction opposes the movement of an object through the air. When an object moves against friction some of its kinetic energy is changed into heat. Friction causes heat to be produced in all energy convertors. Electrical resistance isn't friction but it can be thought of as the force opposing the flow of current through a conductor as it converts electrical energy into heat.

Above: The four stages of a petrol engine. Petrol is sucked in through the opening at the left (induction), compressed by the piston (compression), ignited by the spark plug (power), and finally pushed back out of the right side valve opening (exhaust). Energy is released during the explosion occurring during the power stroke. Chemical energy is here converted into mechanical energy.

Above: The lift-off of Apollo 15 is an example of the conversion of the chemical energy in rocket fuel to the kinetic energy of the moving rocket.

Left: The vacuum cleaner uses a motor to convert electrical energy to mechanical energy.

Energy and life

Energy in food

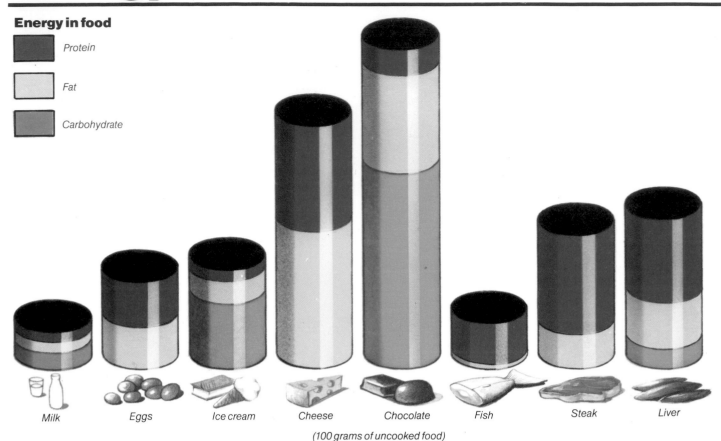

■ Protein

□ Fat

▨ Carbohydrate

Milk   Eggs   Ice cream   Cheese   Chocolate   Fish   Steak   Liver

(100 grams of uncooked food)

On observing the curious light from a firefly, a scientist may not only wonder at its beauty, but will also try to understand the process which allows this tiny insect to produce so much light energy. The conversion of food into energy takes place within microscopic cells in the bodies of all animals.

Energy and man

The energy available from a certain amount of food is measured in kilojoules (kJ). Many slimmers continue to use a unit which is now obsolete, the calorie. One calorie is equivalent to 4.2 kJ (4,200 joules).

A moderately active man has an average daily energy requirement of 12-12,500 kJ, a woman's is much lower at 9-9,500 kJ, a teenage boy 11,500-12,000 kJ, a teenage girl 9,500-10,000 kJ, and a child aged two needs about 5,000 kJ of energy.

Most foods that we eat are a complex mixture of carbohydrates, fats, proteins, vitamins, minerals and, of course, water.

Carbohydrates such as sugar or starch are the body's main source of energy. Sugary foods include chocolate, sweet fruits and toffee, while bread, potatoes and pasta all contain a lot of starch. Many people eat more

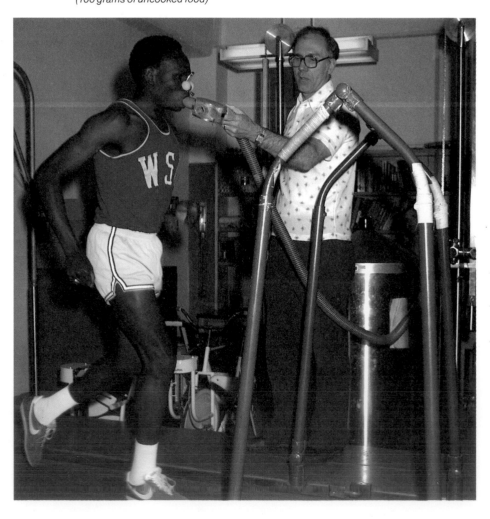

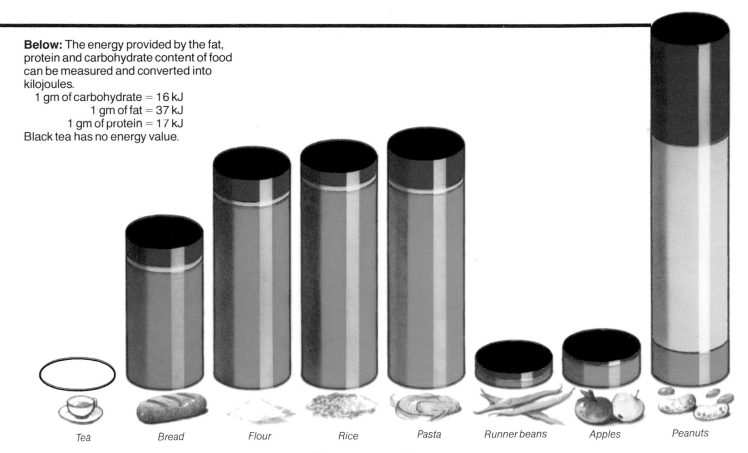

Below: The energy provided by the fat, protein and carbohydrate content of food can be measured and converted into kilojoules.

1 gm of carbohydrate = 16 kJ
1 gm of fat = 37 kJ
1 gm of protein = 17 kJ

Black tea has no energy value.

Tea   Bread   Flour   Rice   Pasta   Runner beans   Apples   Peanuts

(100 grams of uncooked food)

carbohydrates than they need, and these are converted by the body into fat. Although each gram of fat contains twice as much potential energy as one gram of carbohydrate, the conversion of this potential energy into a useful form takes a very long time. To encourage the body to convert some of its excess fat into energy, slimmers often eat foods low in carbohydrates.

Breathing

External respiration is one of the fundamental processes of life. Basically, it involves an organism taking in oxygen from its surroundings. This oxygen is then used to burn up food materials in order to yield energy and the resulting carbon dioxide is expelled as a waste gas. The haemoglobin in red blood cells picks up oxygen in the lungs to form oxyhaemoglobin.

A strong heart and lungs then ensure that a continuous supply of these oxygen-rich blood cells reaches the muscles. For instance, marathon runners must be capable of absorbing a great deal of oxygen and transferring it quickly to their muscles. At the muscles, an energy-producing reaction called 'aerobic respiration' takes place between digested food and oxygen. The bloodstream then transports the carbon dioxide formed in this reaction back to the lungs.

Oxygen debt

The great explosion of energy required for athletic events such as the 100 metres and the discus originates from a quite different reaction known as 'anaerobic respiration'. In this process food is converted, in the absence of oxygen, into lactic acid. A build-up of lactic acid in the muscles prevents them from working properly, and so anaerobic respiration produces energy for only short periods of time. The oxygen taken by an athlete in great gulps at the end of a race is used to convert the lactic acid into harmless products. The volume of oxygen inhaled for this purpose is known as the oxygen debt, and it can take a sprinter anything up to 25 minutes to fully repay his oxygen debt.

Left: The Kenyan athlete Henry Rono in training. Here the doctor is testing the gases which the athlete breathes in and out during running by using a respirometer.

Right: Blood travels to every part of the body. The diagram shows oxygen-rich blood in red and blood with a greater concentration of carbon dioxide in blue.

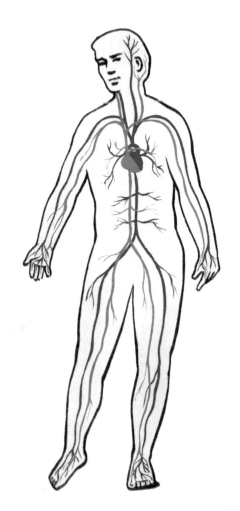

Plants and energy

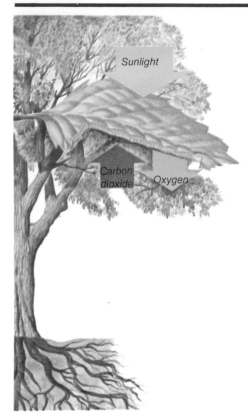

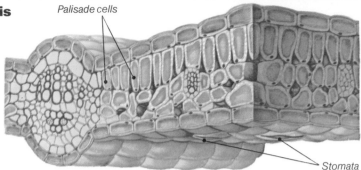

Palisade cells

Stomata

Left and **right:** Green plants can manufacture food from carbon dioxide and water. The energy needed for this manufacturing process comes from sunlight absorbed by the green chemical, chlorophyll, found in leaves. Carbon dioxide is taken in through the pores or stomata of the leaves and water is carried up from the roots in vertical veins called vascular bundles. The process produces oxygen which is passed out through the leaf stomata, and sugar which is stored as starch.

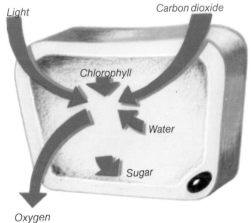

Light

Carbon dioxide

Chlorophyll

Water

Sugar

Oxygen

Below: The Kreen Akorore tribe in the Amazon Basin are here using man's oldest plant fuel, wood, for heat.

Grass is eaten by an antelope which in turn is eaten by a lion. This sequence of events is called a food chain. Every living organism is involved in one or more food chains and every food chain begins with a plant. Food chains are also called energy chains because it is through the various links in these chains that animals get their energy.

Man's place in the natural community could well be described by the simple food chain: grass▶cattle▶man. Such a chain, however, fails to show the many different foods found in man's daily diet. To fully describe the food pattern within any community requires a much more complicated diagram called a food web.

Photosynthesis

Green plants are biological energy convertors, converting the energy from the sun into chemical potential energy and storing it in food materials. Most of this potential energy is contained in a group of compounds called carbohydrates, and the reaction which produces them is known as photosynthesis. Carbohydrates are produced by the combining of carbon dioxide absorbed from the air with water drawn up from the ground through the plant's roots. Animals absorb this energy when they eat

Below: Food webs are often drawn in pyramid shape with plants at the base, herbivores (plant-eaters) in the next layer, and the top layers filled with small and large carnivores (meat-eaters).

Above: The 'sugar' commonly used in foods is sucrose, extracted from sugar cane grown in fields like this one in Mauritius. The plant's sap contains between 10-20 per cent sugar.

Food web

plants; photosynthesis is therefore vital to all life on Earth.

Chlorophyll is the chemical which gives the plant its green colour. Only plants which contain chlorophyll can use light energy in photosynthesis. Photosynthesis produces vast quantities of organic substances – as much as 225,000 million tonnes a year. Over 75 per cent of this is produced by tiny sea plants (phytoplankton).

Biomass and biofuels

Materials which are, or have recently been, plants can often be made into fuels. Such materials are known as biomass, and the fuel produced is called a biofuel. The earliest used and most widespread of all biofuels is wood. Combustion, or burning, is a process which converts the energy of wood into heat and light energy. Wood, however, is a scarce resource which takes many years to mature. Large-scale burning of forests is therefore both an unsuccessful and a short-sighted approach to the solution of man's energy problems. Re-afforestation programmes are a priority where this has occurred in the past.

Most other forms of biomass contain a great deal of moisture and therefore are not suitable for burning. Almost as much energy would be needed to dry these materials as would be released by combustion. Wet biomass such as agricultural, forestry and domestic waste can however be converted into many other high-quality fuels.

Biological processes are already used at sewage works and on farms to convert domestic and agricultural sewage into methane gas. Natural gas is mainly composed of methane, and this process could well be used in the near future to produce quite large quantities of this important fuel. Small amounts of oil have now been produced in the laboratory from domestic rubbish, and it is hoped that large-scale experiments will prove to be equally successful.

Growing plants for fuel is an energy option open to countries with large areas of land not needed for food cultivation. Brazilian cars have been made to run on alcohol made from specially-grown cane sugar and cassava. Industrialized countries which cannot spare the land could satisfy a small but important percentage of their energy needs by converting refuse into biofuels.

Prospecting for fuels

Radioactivity survey

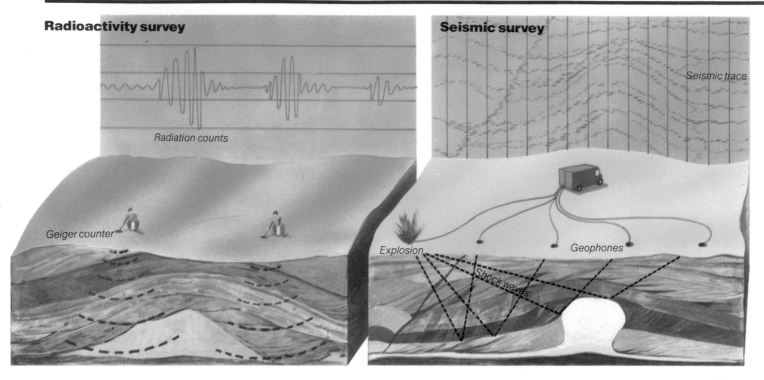

Radiation counts

Geiger counter

Seismic survey

Seismic trace

Explosion

Geophones

Shock waves

Above: Rocks rich in uranium are radioactive. Prospectors use radiation detectors such as geiger counters in their search for underground deposits.

The only sure way to discover whether an area has valuable underground fuel deposits is to drill or dig a hole and see what turns up! In the early days of America's oil boom, prospectors gambled everything on wells which often had little or no chance of success. Today a full geological survey is always carried out before drilling begins.

Detection methods
To discover what lies underground, without actually digging a hole, is a little like guessing the contents of a wrapped present without unwrapping it. You may look at its size, give it a shake, test its weight, and even hold it up to the light. Geologists use a series of slightly more scientific tests to determine what exactly lies beneath our feet.

In a geological survey, large areas are quickly and accurately mapped by aerial photography. From this map a geologist can often deduce a great deal of information about underground rock formations. By collecting fossils and rock samples from selected sites, the geologist can then determine both the age and type of rock shown on the map.

In a geophysical survey, modern scientific instruments provide accurate information about the Earth's physical

Below: This diagram shows a land drilling rig and a cross-section of the rock geology it has drilled through. It is about to break through into an oil and gas reservoir which may possibly be under considerable pressure. During drilling a lubricating 'chemical mud' is pumped down to the bit and returns inside the casing lining. If the rock is particularly hard, several diamond bits can be worn out.

A land oil rig

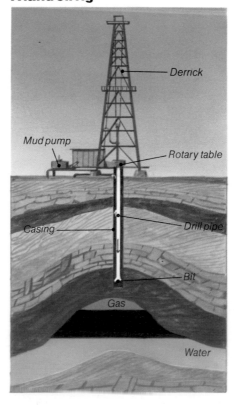

Derrick

Mud pump

Rotary table

Casing

Drill pipe

Bit

Gas

Water

Above: Seismic surveying uses shock waves from an underground explosion to reflect the rock geology. The surface detectors are called geophones.

properties such as its magnetic and gravitational field strength, elasticity, density and degree of radioactivity. These are the tell-tale signs which a geologist uses to identify particular rock layers.

Seismic methods are commonly used by the oil industry both to detect the presence of fuel trapped in rocks and to estimate the thickness of the porous source rocks. Controlled explosions send out shock waves into the Earth's crust and these are reflected back to a series of detectors called geophones. The time taken for the waves to travel back gives information about the rocks encountered on the journey. This information is also used in coal mining to measure the thickness and length of underground coal seams.

Airborne scintillometers have largely taken over from hand-held geiger counters in the search for the radioactivity associated with uranium deposits.

In a geochemical survey soil, plant and water samples are analysed in the hope of detecting tiny traces of elements associated with particular ores. An unusually large percentage of radon (a radioactive gas formed from radium) often indicates a source of uranium nearby.

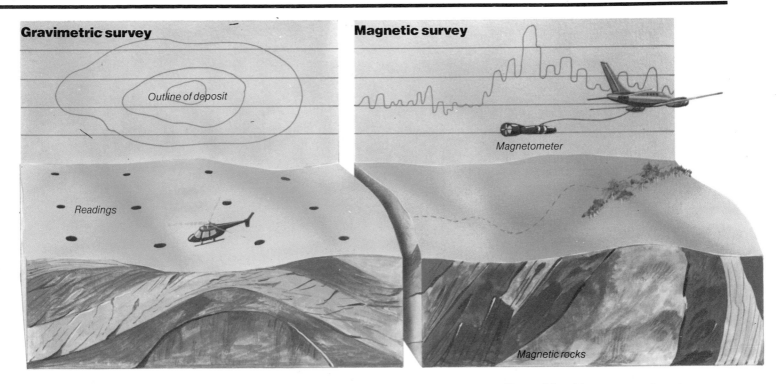

Gravimetric survey

Outline of deposit

Readings

Magnetic survey

Magnetometer

Magnetic rocks

Above: A gravimetric survey measures the strength of the Earth's gravitational field. The readings here indicate the presence of an anticline.

Below: Oil-bearing rocks consist of tiny particles separated by air spaces. The smaller the pore size of the rock, the lower the percentage of extractable oil.

Above: The airborne magnetometer detects slight changes in the Earth's magnetic field. Volcanic rocks are more strongly magnetic than sedimentary rocks.

Not all of our coal, oil and gas deposits occur beneath the land surface. The rocks beneath the sea bed are becoming an increasingly important source. Coal seams in coastal areas may even extend out beneath the sea bed. Prospecting is much more difficult in these conditions.

Rock formations

Oil and gas tend to seep upwards through tiny spaces or pores in overlying rocks until they are stopped by a more solid 'cap' rock. The fuel 'trap' is complete when a particular rock formation halts the oil or gas in its sideways progress through the porous source rock. Oil and gas are mostly found in sedimentary rocks such as sandstone and limestone.

Oil companies use geophysical methods to look for special rock formations capable of trapping oil and gas. Common traps such as faults, anticlines and salt domes cause changes in the Earth's magnetic and gravitational fields. An airborne magnetometer can often detect the presence of the more magnetic trap rocks. Salt domes near the surface cause a slight reduction in the Earth's gravitational field and this can be measured by the very sensitive gravimeter.

Oil and gas geology

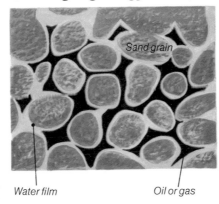

Sand grain

Water film   *Oil or gas*

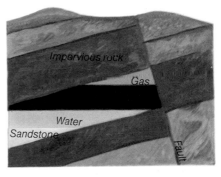

Impervious rock

Gas

Water

Sandstone

Fault

A fault trap is an oil and gas reservoir that occurs when rocks are tilted and then faulted by movements of the Earth.

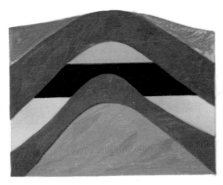

An anticline is the most usual reservoir, caused by an upfold in the rocks. It creates an underground dome or ridge.

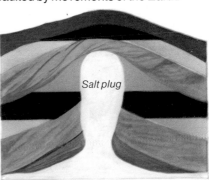

Salt plug

Salt domes are bodies of salt forced up from deep underground which raise the overlying rocks into a dome shape.

Coal and peat

Coal mine

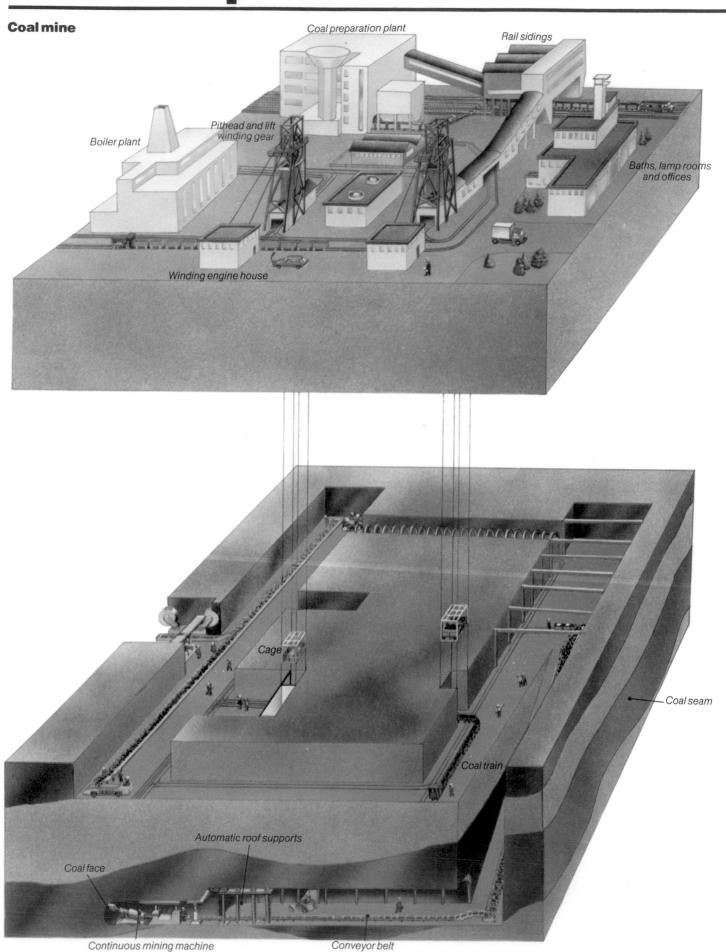

Coal preparation plant

Rail sidings

Boiler plant

Pithead and lift winding gear

Baths, lamp rooms and offices

Winding engine house

Cage

Coal seam

Coal train

Automatic roof supports

Coal face

Continuous mining machine

Conveyor belt

The story of coal begins in the Carboniferous Period some 300 million years before man first walked on the Earth. During this period the Earth was covered with dense forests, swamps and rivers, and luxuriant vegetation. A thick mat of dead plant material gradually formed which later decayed and became immersed in the acid waters of the surrounding swamps. A restricted supply of oxygen prevented the attacking bacteria from completely decomposing the submerged plant material. Slowly, over a period of millions of years, countless tons of earth and rock compressed and altered the dead vegetation.

With increasing heat and pressure the dead vegetation formed peat. The peat became lignite (brown coal), and this hardened first to bituminous coal before, finally, the energy-rich anthracite coal was formed. Generally, the greater the heat and pressure the higher the percentage of pure carbon in the coal. Peat has a carbon content of approximately 60 per cent and an energy value of less than 14 MJ per kilogram, whereas anthracite has 94 per cent carbon content and an energy value of over 30.

Coal mining

There are two types of coal mine, opencast and shaft. Opencast mining is suitable for surface seams where the overlying soil and rock are simply stripped off the top to get at the coal. Where the seams lie deeper, shaft mining is used. Miners now have at their disposal a vast army of machines to assist them in their difficult task. Giant trepanning machines gouge into the coal face, throwing tons of coal into a conveyor belt at the rear. As the cutter advances, the roof is supported by hyd-

Coal tar by-products

Soap and detergents

Linoleum

Perfume

Battery electrolyte

Fertilizers

Ink

Paint

Adhesives

Plastics

Nylon

Above: A range of products made from coal tar. This formerly large industry has become

raulic pit props automatically adjusting to suit the load they have to bear.

Formerly, opencast mines were a great eyesore on the landscape. Now, as the mechanical diggers cut out the coal, it is possible for huge mechanical shovels to restore the original topsoil and quickly return the area to normal.

Coal products

Over the past few decades coal's share of the world energy market has gradually been lost to the oil and gas industry. Many former coal tar products are now in fact oil-derived. By the year 2000 this trend will probably be reversed as more and more coal is converted into different fuels. Britain and America are co-operating in the development of the

much less important due to the wider use of oil as a petrochemical feedstock.

COGAS process which converts coal to liquid fuels and substitute natural gas. South Africa has been converting coal to petrol since 1955, and now obtains 30 per cent of its petrol in this way.

World reserves

Estimates of world coal reserves vary considerably. As fuels become more expensive and technology advances, it becomes economic to mine coal that was previously thought to be unusable through location or thinness of seams. It is thought that the USA has about 31 per cent of the world's known recoverable reserves of 652 billion tonnes. The USSR may have about 23 per cent, Western Europe 18 per cent, and China around 14 per cent.

Left: The layout of a modern coal mine. Above ground, the buildings in the background are for washing, sorting and grading the coal. Miners descend in one lift-cage whilst the other carries coal to the surface. At the very bottom of the page a giant coal-cutting machine can be seen working at the coal face. Behind the machine trails a conveyor belt which carries the coal to a higher level. Automatic pit props can be seen supporting the roof to the rear of the coal-cutting machine.

Right: Peat drying in the Hebrides. In Ireland this traditional fuel is a major source of industrial energy.

Oil

About half of the energy used in the world today comes from oil. This modern storehouse of chemical energy was formed millions of years ago from the remains of tiny sea creatures called plankton. As the plankton died they slowly formed a thick carpet of organic material on the sea bed. Bacteria feeding on these remains began its transformation into oil and gas. Heat and pressure from overlying rocks completed it over many millions of years.

Drilling for oil

Once a survey is done, a test well is drilled using a rotating shaft at the end of which is a drill bit. This is connected to a drill platform at the surface. As the shaft drives deeper, the hole is lined with steel piping. The rock fragments are washed out with water and soft clay. This 'chemical mud', pumped down the inside of the drill pipes, also controls the oil pressure and cools the bit.

When the drill bit reaches an oil reservoir, because the fluid is under pressure, the oil may come out as a gusher. A set of valves known as a christmas tree is placed at the well head to control the flow of oil and prevent such a 'blowout'. If the oil is found in commercial quantities, then a more permanent production platform replaces the drilling rig.

Refining oil

The refinery is a vast industrial complex which separates, breaks down and recombines the crude oil into six main types of fuel. The refining process begins with the distillation, or separation, of heavy crude oil in a large tower called a fractionating column. Petroleum gases, such as butane and propane, and low boiling liquids rise to the top of the column while the higher-boiling oils and tars remain lower down. Fractions or cuts are then drawn off at different heights on the column, dependent upon the boiling point of the fraction.

This process does not yield enough of the lighter oils so the heavier oils are

Right: The crude oil is first heated to its boiling point of about 400°C before being transferred to the bottom of this fractionating tower. Lines of trays together with the semi-circular 'bubble cups' prevent the oil vapours from rising too quickly. When a gas reaches a tray which is at its boiling point it condenses to a liquid and is drawn off.

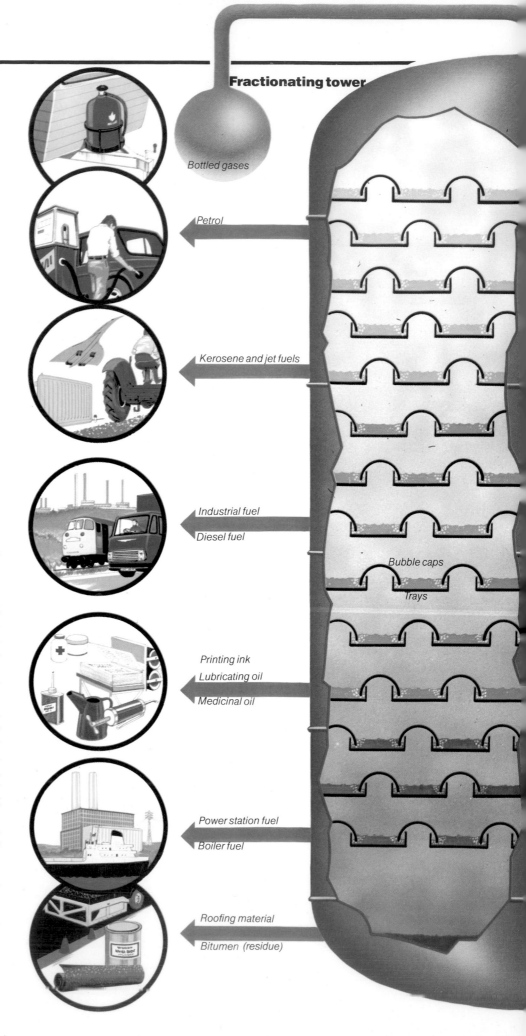

Fractionating tower

Bottled gases

Petrol

Kerosene and jet fuels

Industrial fuel

Diesel fuel

Bubble caps

Trays

Printing ink

Lubricating oil

Medicinal oil

Power station fuel

Boiler fuel

Roofing material

Bitumen (residue)

Heated crude oil

again heated but this time under pressure to form lighter oils. This process is known as cracking. The oil is then blended to give the different octane ratings of petrol.

Oil products

The major refinery products are bitumen, waxes, lubricating oils, diesel fuel, paraffin (kerosene), aviation fuel, petrol and bottled gases.

Bitumen is a dark, waterproof, sticky substance which is a solid at normal temperatures. These properties make it a useful material for binding together the hard rock fragments used in road surfacing.

Paraffin waxes are used to make candles, waterproof food cartons, electrical insulators, polishes and even to pluck poultry.

Liquid fuel fractions such as diesel, aviation fuel and petrol, provide the energy for many forms of transport, while liquefied gases such as butane are commonly supplied in pressurized 'bottles' for use in domestic heating and cooking.

Below: This is one of the world's few reserves of natural pitch. Whilst not an energy source, this lake in Trinidad has

World reserves

Just over 55 per cent of the world's known oil reserves are located in the Middle East belt which stretches from North Africa to Iran.

In the future, increasing scarcity may make it economic to extract oil using more costly methods. As little as 20 per cent of the oil is often extracted from oil reservoirs. The rest of the oil is left trapped in the porous source rocks when the pressure of the accompanying natural gas becomes insufficient to force the oil to the surface. In the North Sea secondary production techniques, such as injecting high pressure water or re-injecting the natural gas, have resulted in the recovery of as much as 45 per cent of the estimated reserves.

Oil shales and tar sands contain thick heavy oil which cannot be extracted by normal methods. Usually they have to be dug out of the ground and then heated to produce the oil. Although it takes at least a tonne of oil shale to produce a barrel of oil, its successful exploitation could double the world's present usable oil reserves.

provided over 15 million tonnes for road surfacing purposes which would otherwise have had to be distilled from oil.

Gas

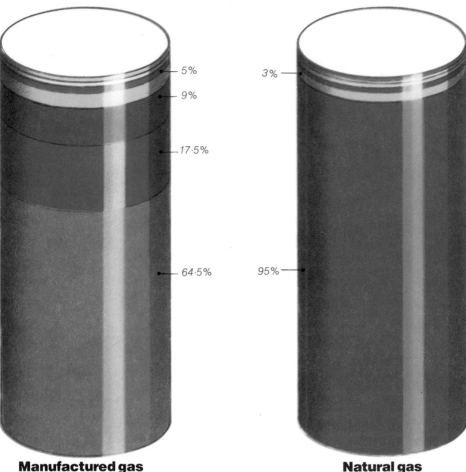

5%
9%
17·5%
64·5%

Manufactured gas

3%
95%

Natural gas

 Carbon dioxide
Carbon monoxide
 Hydrogen
 Methane
 Ethane
 Propane
 Nitrogen
 Butane

Left: Natural gas is usually found along with underground oil deposits. The other gas is manufactured from coal. Natural gas contains no poisonous carbon monoxide and is almost entirely clean burning methane. Scientists are now able to manufacture a gas from coal that is similar in composition to real natural gas. It is called substitute natural gas.

It is difficult to believe that solid metal can actually turn into a gas, but any substance can be solid, liquid or gas dependent upon its temperature and pressure. At normal atmospheric pressure, iron would be a gas at 2800°C while solid oxygen occurs at –219°C. Many fuels exist as gases under normal temperatures and pressures.

Natural gas

Natural gas describes the many different mixtures of fuel gases which are to be found trapped in underground rocks. Its history is long and colourful. In the 3rd century AD the Chinese reportedly used hollow bamboo poles to pipe natural gas from underground reservoirs as part of their salt industry. Today, large production platforms operate diamond-studded drills day and night in order to reach natural gas supplies trapped up to 3,000 metres below the Earth's surface.

Natural gas is composed mainly of methane and is clean burning and non-poisonous. Countries such as Algeria which export large quantities of natural gas have built plants to liquefy the gas before transportation. Liquefied natural gas is distributed around the world in refrigerated tankers.

Iran, the USSR and North America have the largest proven reserves. The discovery in 1959 of huge quantities of natural gas at Schlochteren in north-east Holland prompted a great deal of exploratory drilling in the North Sea.

In the United Kingdom the majority of consumers now receive natural gas through a distribution network that is directly linked by underwater pipeline to North Sea production platforms. But even today many oil companies 'flare off' (burn) this precious fuel because it may not be as commercially profitable as the oil.

Left: The *Methania* carries liquefied natural gas. Refrigerated containers store the gas as a liquid because it then occupies a much smaller volume than the original gas.

Manufactured gases

The coal gas which once made up a large percentage of domestic gas supplies was manufactured by distilling coal. Today many better processes are available for converting both coal and oil into the cleaner and more efficient substitute natural gas.

Butane and propane are produced by distilling oil, and can be conveniently stored as liquids at normal temperatures in pressurized containers.

The hydrogen economy

Over the next 50 years our limited supplies of oil and natural gas will become increasingly scarcer. Even if there is sufficient total energy available from coal, nuclear or other sources to fire the large power stations, this may not be in a form that is suitable for use in cars, buses and planes.

One answer may be to manufacture hydrogen. Although hydrogen is not a naturally-occurring fuel, manufactured hydrogen could store the energy from power stations in a very conven-

ient form for practical use.

The process involved would pass electricity through ordinary water, thus separating the hydrogen from the oxygen. And, given the necessary technology, the hydrogen thus produced could make an excellent fuel for cars and planes and could even provide domestic and industrial heating.

Above: The ancient Chinese were amongst the first to realize the potential of natural gas. It is used here to evaporate salt.

Below: One of the pipe-laying barges that have linked the rigs in the North Sea to the British mainland by pipeline.

Pipe-laying barge

Stinger

Pipe

Nuclear fuels

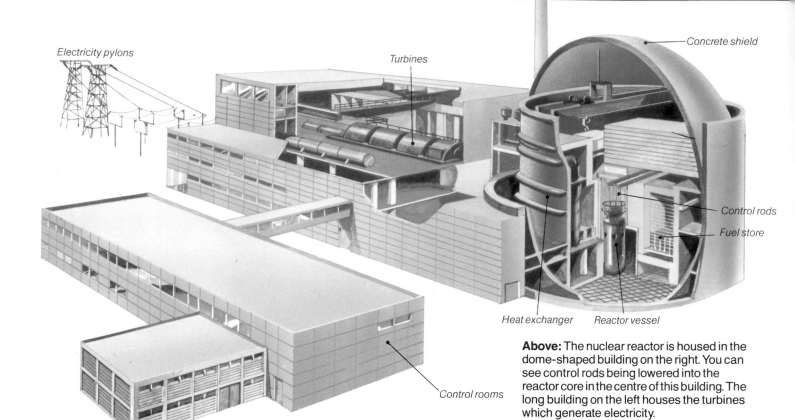

Electricity pylons

Turbines

Concrete shield

Control rods

Fuel store

Heat exchanger

Reactor vessel

Control rooms

Above: The nuclear reactor is housed in the dome-shaped building on the right. You can see control rods being lowered into the reactor core in the centre of this building. The long building on the left houses the turbines which generate electricity.

In 1905 Albert Einstein, then working in the Swiss Patent Office, revolutionized scientific thinking by publishing a paper on the subject of relativity.

According to Einstein, energy and matter are different forms of the same thing. Energy (E) can be converted into matter of mass (m), and back again, according to the now famous equation $E = mc^2$, where c is the speed of light. The equation basically shows that a little matter is equivalent to an enormous amount of energy.

Atomic theory

At the centre of each of the atoms that make up all matter is a tiny nucleus composed of even smaller particles called protons and neutrons. The number of protons in the nucleus of an element never varies and is called the atomic number of the element.

An element may have a number of different forms called isotopes. Each isotope has a particular number of neutrons. The number of protons and neutrons together is called the mass number of the isotope. A uranium nucleus has 92 protons. There are two main uranium isotopes. One has 146 neutrons, giving it a mass number of 238 – hence uranium 238. Whereas uranium 235 has only 143 neutrons.

Thermal reactors

When a free neutron strikes a uranium 235 nucleus at the correct speed, the nucleus disintegrates into two smaller nucleii. In doing so, both energy and two free neutrons are released. If these neutrons can be made to split other uranium 235 nucleii, then the resulting 'chain reaction' of splitting nucleii produces a great deal of energy. This nuc-

lear reaction is called fission. If uncontrolled, all the nucleii in a piece of uranium split in a fraction of a second and this causes a devastating explosion. But if the reaction is controlled in a reactor it provides a steady heat supply.

Chain reactions rarely occur naturally because 99.3 per cent of natural uranium is the stable isotope 238 which harmlessly absorbs neutrons.

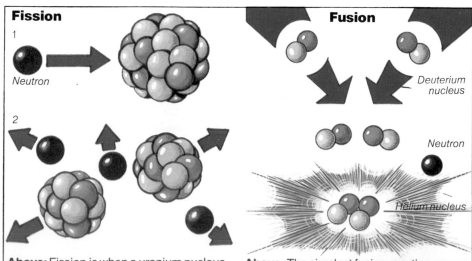

Fission

1

Neutron

2

Fusion

Deuterium nucleus

Neutron

Helium nucleus

Above: Fission is when a uranium nucleus captures a neutron (1). It divides and three neutrons and freeing energy. this reaction may then split other uranium nucleii, so releasing more energy.

Above: The simplest fusion reaction occurs when the nucleii of two atoms of deuterium combine to form the nucleus of a helium atom. This reaction releases an enormous amount of energy.

The chain reaction of the uranium fuel in the reactor core is controlled by control rods made of neutron-absorbing substances such as cadmium. By raising or lowering the rods into the fuel mass, the number of neutrons available for fission is regulated.

In order to increase the likelihood of the free neutrons striking a uranium-235 nucleus, thermal reactors are fuelled by slightly 'enriched' uranium containing a bigger percentage of the 235 isotope.

Fast breeder reactors

The chain reaction is sustained inside a fast breeder reactor without the use of moderators (substances that slow down the 'fast neutrons'). Fast breeders use liquid metals such as sodium as a coolant, and are capable of using spent fuel from thermal reactors. Their one big advantage is that they produce plutonium from the original 'enriched' uranium fuel. This can be reused as a reactor fuel. Most fast breeder reactors are still at the prototype stage as their safety is causing concern.

Nuclear fusion

At temperatures approaching 4 million °C, individual nuclei can be made to join together or fuse. Often this results in mass being converted into energy. The enormous amount of energy released by exploding a hydrogen bomb is a result of the nuclear fusion of two atoms of deuterium, an isotope of hydrogen.

Above: The ghostly blue colour is called Cerenkov radiation and originates from the spent uranium fuel rods.

Below: Three stages in a 'chain reaction'. 1. A uranium nucleus fissions, releasing releases energy (2). The neutrons freed in 2. Some of the free neutrons are captured by other uranium nucleii to produce an even greater number of neutrons.
3. More and more uranium nucleii fission in the 'sea' of free neutrons. In a reactor, millions of these fissions occur every second.

The result of an uncontrolled chain reaction can be seen in this atomic test in Nevada, USA.

Chain reaction

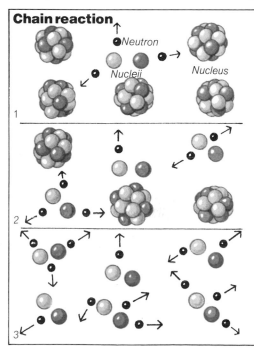

Neutron

Nucleii

Nucleus

1

2

3

Energy conservation at home

All countries waste a great deal of energy by using it inefficiently or unnecessarily. Energy conservation is about stopping this waste.

About 30 per cent of all energy consumed in Western Europe is used in the home, and heating accounts for 60 per cent of this total. In the rest of the world domestic energy consumption depends very much on climate. Generally, in hot countries, air conditioning is a luxury which only the wealthy can afford. Less expensive measures include whitewashing buildings to reflect the Sun's rays and having thick walls to slow down the rate of heat flow from the outside.

Heat flow

Energy in the form of heat travels from higher to lower temperature regions by three very different methods (radiation, convection, and conduction). Infra-red radiation is similar to light and travels through space as a wave motion. Heat flows upwards through liquids and gases by convection while conduction is mainly to do with heat transfer through solids. All metals are good conductors of heat. Common poor conductors (or insulators) include polystyrene, air and pure water.

Preventing heat losses

The heat-conducting properties of different insulators are measured on a scale of 'U values' ranging from 0 to 5. The lower the 'U value' the better the insulator. In Sweden strict building controls demand a maximum 'U value' for outside walls of 0.3, the USA requires about 0.6, while Britain is satisfied with a 'U value' of only 1.

To prevent dampness seeping through from the outside most new houses have two separate walls. Heat losses can be reduced by filling the cavity (space) between them with an insulating material such as polystyrene foam. Great care must be taken to ensure that 'cavity wall insulation' does not allow moisture to seep through to the inside wall.

Convection currents carrying heat upwards cause heat to be lost through the roof. A 100 millimetre thick layer of insulating material on the floor of the loft can cut heat loss by 50 per cent.

On sunny days south-facing windows can absorb quite a lot of solar energy, whereas heat energy normally escapes through the windows. Double glazing is an effective, though costly, solution to this problem.

The flow of air in and out of a house is called ventilation, and is usually measured in air changes per hour (ac/h). Ventilation also removes moisture from the inside of a house, and a minimum natural ventilation of about 1ac/h is needed to prevent the build-up of condensation. Stopping draughts around

Above: Air is an excellent heat insulator. The layer of air trapped between the two panes of glass reduces the amount of heat escaping through the windows.

Above: Cavity wall insulation is when insulating foam is injected into the space between the inside and outside walls of a building.

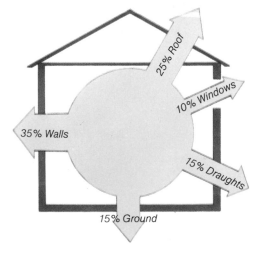

35% Walls
25% Roof
10% Windows
15% Draughts
15% Ground

Above: This diagram shows the typical heat losses from a poorly insulated house in a temperate climate.

Left: This picture was taken with a film specially sensitive to infra-red (heat) radiation. The warmer colours (reds and yellows) show where the greatest amount of heat is escaping.

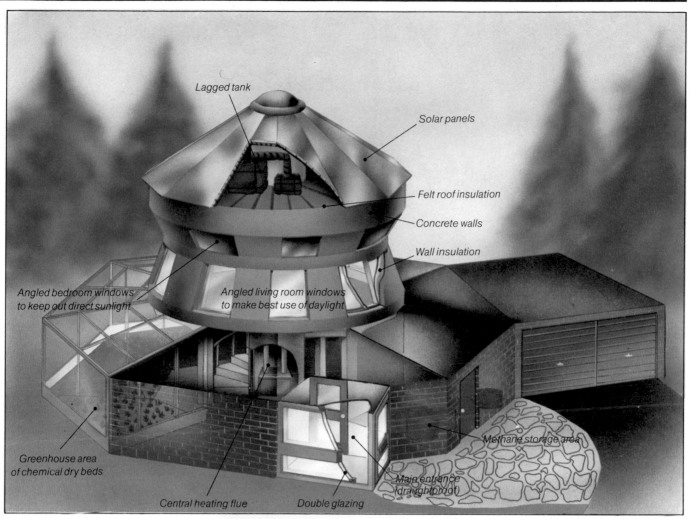

Lagged tank

Solar panels

Felt roof insulation

Concrete walls

Wall insulation

Angled bedroom windows
to keep out direct sunlight

Angled living room windows
to make best use of daylight

Methane storage area

Greenhouse area
of chemical dry beds

Central heating flue

Double glazing

Main entrance
(draughtproof)

Above: This is an artist's impression of a 'house of the future' incorporating several energy conserving ideas.

Right: These houses on the Greek island of Santorini are painted white to reflect the Sun's rays. Their thick walls reduce the flow of heat both in and out of the houses.

doors and windows can reduce the ventilation rate to this value, and is one of the cheapest and most effective ways of reducing heat losses. No amount of insulation is effective if ventilation is greater than 3 ac/h.

Clothing

The insulating properties of clothing can be classified on a scale of values ranging from 0 (no clothes) to 4 (Arctic clothing). People wearing lightweight suits with a value of 1 are comfortable at temperatures around 22°C. Long underwear, a heavy three-piece suit and woollen socks raise the value to about 1.5, and reduce the 'comfort' temperature to nearer 18°C. A willingness to wear clothing of this sort indoors could reduce energy consumption by up to 30 per cent.

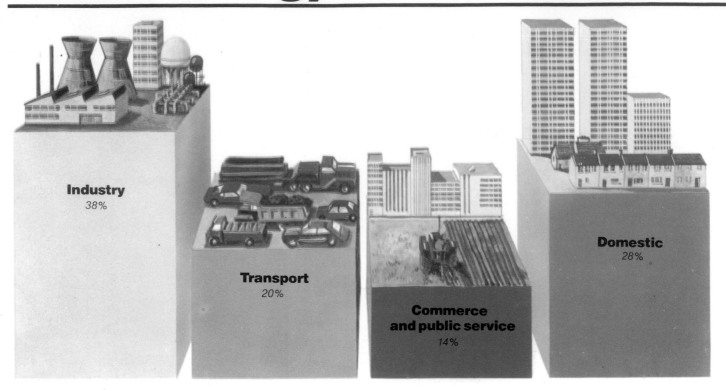

Industry
38%

Transport
20%

Commerce
and public service
14%

Domestic
28%

Above: The energy consumption figures for the majority of industrialized European countries are all very similar. The data here relates to the UK, France, Sweden, Holland and West Germany.

Below: The Mitsui building in Tokyo is a huge glass building that must be impossible to insulate. To keep these workers cool in summer and warm in winter requires a great deal of energy.

Energy sources are finite and precious and are now being rapidly used up. Industrialized countries have squandered energy in the past, sometimes at the expense of less developed countries. Since 1973, when oil supplies from the Middle East were severely disrupted and massive price increases were announced by the producers, the tables have been turned. Industrialized countries have now become aware of the need to save energy. The rocketing price of oil has played havoc with their economic budgeting.

Every country, even the energy-rich, can play its part in making sure that no form of energy is ever wasted. Countries with natural 'renewable' sources could exploit them to the full so that the energy-poor countries can have a greater share of the scarcer fuels. Norway already satisfies about 70 per cent of its energy needs from hydro-electricity. Other countries such as Greece, France, West Germany and Japan depend to a much larger extent on imported oil.

Transport

Most industrialized countries use about 20 per cent of their oil for transport, but in America the proportion is closer to 60 per cent. The lack of public transport and their huge 'gas-guzzling' cars can claim some responsibility for this high figure.

Today, car manufacturers are being

forced to perfect the energy-saving car. The air resistance of a particular car greatly affects both its performance and its petrol consumption. Wind tunnel tests show that modern 'wedge-shaped' cars have a particularly low wind resistance.

One of the most exciting modern developments in car design has been the invention of the 'in-car computer'. It can easily be programmed to display petrol consumption. A new BMW even has a mini computer which automatically adjusts the timing of the engine 100 times every second. Developments such as these will greatly improve engine efficiency and hence reduce fuel consumption.

Many fuels can be shown to be more efficient than petrol. Recent tests have shown that a hydrogen-powered car is 50 per cent more efficient than a petrol engine. However, hydrogen is not a primary fuel and is itself expensive to produce.

Electric engines are quiet, efficient and non-polluting but the problem of storing enough electrical energy for a long journey and the weight and expense of the battery itself seem at present to prevent this type of transport from becoming popular. However, a major breakthrough in battery design could alter this.

Under normal conditions diesel engines can use between 35 and 40 per cent less fuel than similar petrol engines. This economy and engine durability has to be offset against its disadvantages: it is dirty, noisy, and the power unit is heavier and more expensive. Overall it gives a much lower power output.

Industry

Much energy is wasted in offices, factories and public buildings by people not bothering to switch off lights or regulate heating. About 15 per cent of British electricity is consumed in lighting offices and at home.

Industrial processes often generate a great deal of heat. Waste heat recovery systems use this heat energy either for heating purposes or to generate electricity. One British electricity generating board is building a combined heat and power station at Hereford in the Midlands. Two diesel engines will generate electricity to feed the public supply system and the surplus heat produced in the process will be supplied to heat nearby factories.

Streamlining

Interrupted flow

Streamlined flow

Energy policies

Governments can encourage energy conservation by educating the public and by supplying grants for energy-saving measures. However, the fact remains that the introduction of higher fuel prices remains the most effective, if not the most popular, method of encouraging energy conservation.

Above: The Morris Minor at the top presents a greater resistance to the flow of air. Streamlining can greatly reduce fuel consumption, especially at high speeds.

Below: Industrial processes usually produce a lot of waste heat. The Vasterås combined heat and power station in Sweden has been designed to harness this wasted energy.

How much does it cost?

From the oilfields of Prudhoe Bay, 350 kilometres inside the Arctic Circle, to the oil terminal and Alaskan port of Valdez, is 1,250 kilometres of the coldest and most inhospitable territory known. The Trans-Alaskan pipeline, built to connect the two places, crosses three mountain ranges and 20 rivers. But the $9,000 million spent on constructing this pipeline forms only a small part of an oil company's development costs.

Every new oilfield presents its own special problems. The heavy oil in the Orinoco basin in South America is difficult to extract and when refined is not good quality. The cold weather and rough seas make high-quality North Sea oil expensive to produce.

Prices

The final price of oil is not, however, based upon production costs alone. About half of the world's oil comes from countries who are members of the Organization of Petroleum Exporting Countries (OPEC), and it is this organization which largely fixes the world price of oil. As fuel reserves dry up, the OPEC countries must try to maintain their high income for as long as possible. In recent years some of these countries have reduced production to conserve their dwindling reserves. Reducing production also keeps oil scarce and increases its market value.

The UK is now a net exporter of oil, although not a member of OPEC. By

For just one unit of electricity ...

A blender makes 500 pints of soup

A kettle boils 12 pints of water

A fridge will work for a day

A drill can be used for 2-4 hours

A 1 kilowatt fan heater will provide an hour's warmth

A toaster will make 70 slices of toast

A 2 kilowatt convector heater will provide ½ hour's warmth

Fuel efficiency

1985 the British government expects an annual income of around £4,000 million from North Sea oil taxes. This figure represents nearly 80 per cent of all the money earned from North Sea oil. The remaining £1,000 million will be shared each year amongst the oil-producing companies.

Generating electricity

Electricity is convenient and practical but cannot be dug out of the ground. Any energy source mentioned in this book can be used to generate electricity, but the cost differs for each source.

Renewable energy sources are sometimes looked upon as 'free' energy, but although there is no fuel to pay for, a

Left: This diagram compares the heat energy produced by burning one gram of solid or liquid fuel and one cubic metre of gas, but on different scales. The uranium 235 used here is from a thermal reactor.

36

A food mixer will mix 60 cakes

An iron can be used for 2 hours

A coffee percolator will make 75 cups

A shaver will give over 1800 shaves

A 60 watt reading lamp will last for 16·5 hours

A tumble drier will provide 30 minutes' drying time

A vacuum cleaner can be used for 2-4 hours

Left: This chart gives some idea of the running costs of some domestic appliances in terms of use per unit of electricity. Notice how little time you get for a fan heater or spin dryer, compared to a fridge.

from nuclear sources far outweigh any price advantages.

Energy budgeting

Electrical appliances are rated according to their power consumption. This is measured in watts, or kilowatts (1,000 watts). Electricity bills are calculated according to the number of units recorded by the electricity meter. The electricity board's unit of electricity is the kilowatt hour. This is the energy used by a 1kW appliance in one hour. An automatic washing machine is usually rated at 3kW. This results in a bill of 3 units for every hour of continuous operation. On the other hand, the same three units could keep five 60 watt light bulbs burning for 10 hours.

Heating appliances are particularly expensive to run. A two-bar electric fire could easily use 12 units in one night. Many people try to reduce heating costs by insulating their homes. Draught-proofing and hot water tank insulation can pay for themselves within a year but it can take up to 20 years to recover money spent on double glazing.

Below: Here the Trans-Alaskan pipeline is carried on stilts to prevent the warm oil melting the permafrost. The pipeline was opened on 1 August 1977.

great deal of money must be spent in setting up the generating equipment. At present only hydroelectricity can compete in terms of cost with the traditional fuels.

Large-scale generation of electricity from renewable sources would require hundreds of windmills, hectares of solar cells or many kilometres of wave energy convertors. The setting-up costs are staggering and the running costs might prove high too. Although initially the Rance estuary tidal power station produced electricity which was dearer than more conventional means, it now works out a cheaper source.

Nuclear power stations are also expensive to build but fairly cheap to operate. One unit of electricity from a nuclear power station can possibly be produced for around 60 per cent of the cost of generating it in other power stations. However, people fear that the risks involved in generating electricity

Risks

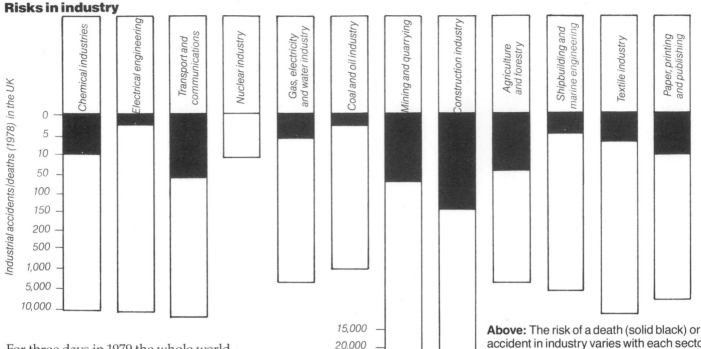

Industrial accidents/deaths (1978) in the UK

Chemical industries

Electrical engineering

Transport and communications

Nuclear industry

Gas, electricity and water industry

Coal and oil industry

Mining and quarrying

Construction industry

Agriculture and forestry

Shipbuilding and marine engineering

Textile industry

Paper, printing and publishing

0
5
10
50
100
150
200
500
1,000
5,000
10,000

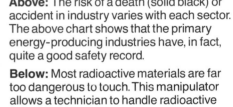

15,000
20,000
25,000
30,000
35,000
40,000
45,000

Above: The risk of a death (solid black) or accident in industry varies with each sector. The above chart shows that the primary energy-producing industries have, in fact, quite a good safety record.

Below: Most radioactive materials are far too dangerous to touch. This manipulator allows a technician to handle radioactive substances in safety.

For three days in 1979 the whole world watched and waited as American engineers fought desperately to prevent a major escape of radioactivity from the Three Mile Island nuclear power station. In the event there was no major serious leak, but the publicity surrounding the accident has fuelled the serious doubts about nuclear safety. In fact, there is still a danger of a leak of radioactive coolant because the reactor has had to be kept under pressure due to the residual supply of heat in the core.

Radioactivity

A major element in the fear of nuclear power is that if an accident occurs it might be very serious indeed. Nuclear power stations produce highly dangerous radioactive materials which emit three types of radiation: *alpha, beta,* and *gamma.* All radioactive materials must be treated with a great deal of care but it is the *gamma* sources which are the most dangerous.

Gamma radiation penetrating the body damages living cells and may cause cancer and leukaemia. A person exposed to the radiation may not be even aware of it until the disease is diagnosed some years later. In addition, one of the nuclear fuels is the highly poisonous plutonium.

Gamma radiation travels long distances through air and can even penetrate thick lead or concrete. All radioactive substances are therefore shielded with a sufficient thickness of material to prevent the escape of these

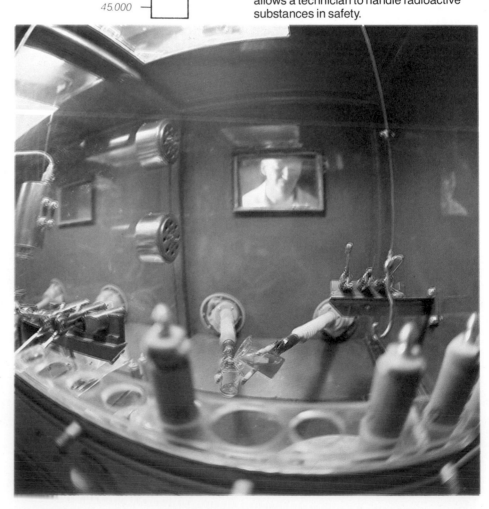

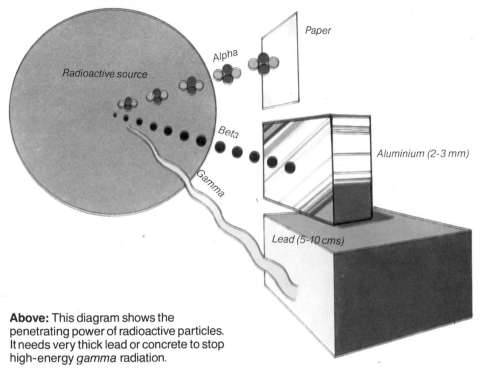

Paper

Alpha

Radioactive source

Beta

Aluminium (2-3 mm)

Gamma

Lead (5-10 cms)

Above: This diagram shows the penetrating power of radioactive particles. It needs very thick lead or concrete to stop high-energy *gamma* radiation.

harmful rays. Measuring instruments such as geiger counters can be used to check the amount of radiation coming from any source.

The possibility of a nuclear explosion at a reactor is remote, but overheating is a very real danger. Although safety systems are often doubled (and even tripled), Three Mile Island shows that accidents can happen.

Many people fear that terrorists could steal enough radioactive material to manufacture a crude atomic bomb. To prevent this from happening, very strict security measures are enforced at all nuclear power stations.

Finally, the waste material produced is also radioactive, and remains so for a very long time. Nuclear scientists are confident that this waste material can be safely stored thousands of metres underground. But few people are happy about having a nuclear dump nearby. Alternatively, nuclear power could be an inexpensive route to a very large source of energy.

Other energy hazards

Petrol tankers in city streets, 400,000 volt cables above our heads, explosive gases piped to millions of homes – these are but a few of the many risks we take for granted. We tolerate these very real dangers because we value the benefits. Yet every year gas explosions and electric shocks account for many deaths.

For some it is their job to brave the extremes of danger in the constant search for our precious fuels. Coal miners, North Sea divers, and oil rig workers are only a small part of the long list of people who take special risks to keep the world supplied with fuel.

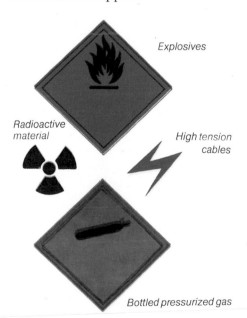

Explosives

Radioactive material

High tension cables

Bottled pressurized gas

Above: Some common hazard warning signs are shown here.

Right: This large oil tanker blew up whilst off-loading its crude oil cargo at the oil terminal in picturesque Bantry Bay, Ireland.

Pollution

Above: There are 27 ways in the above picture that man pollutes the Earth. They can be divided into three categories: atmospheric pollution, pollution of the land, and of water. The vast majority are energy-related. First, try and spot as many as you can, then turn to page 47 for a more detailed analysis.

Pollution is the contamination of the air, land, rivers, lakes and seas with harmful materials as a result of man's activities. Pollutants (materials which pollute the environment) range from household rubbish to the waste from factories and car exhausts. They can make buildings dirty, people's eyes sting, spoil a landscape, foul a waterway, and pose a serious threat to health.

Today people are becoming more aware of these problems and often form 'action groups' to oppose the unnecessary spoiling of the Earth we live on.

Atmospheric pollution

All the millions of tonnes of coal burned throughout the world every day end up either in the atmosphere as gas or as waste. In America, coal is burned at an average rate of 913 million tonnes a minute. In the time taken to read this sentence another 15 tonnes of coal waste will have accumulated. Smoke, grit, sulphur, carbon dioxide and soot are all pumped into the atmosphere, and the remaining coal ash is dumped as solid waste.

Modern power station chimneys use filtering devices known as 'arresters' to remove much of the grit and dust by-products of burning fuel. These chimneys are so high that most of the remaining gases flow straight into the upper atmosphere without ever being inhaled by man. Unfortunately, this means that the upper atmosphere becomes polluted also. Scientists are particularly worried about the increased concentration of carbon dioxide here. Any increase in this gas could limit the escape of heat from the Earth below. No-one can be sure what effect this will have on our climate, but it is always dangerous to disturb nature's sensitive balance.

Oil spills

One of the consequences of man's pres-

ent dependence on oil is the destruction of beaches, marine life and birds by giant oil slicks. With so many large tankers sailing to every corner of the globe it is inevitable that some accidents occasionally occur. Even so, greater care taken by tanker operators would ensure that oil slicks never occur as a result of carelessness.

When a slick is sighted a whole team of experts move into action. First, the extent of the slick is assessed and its probable course plotted. Experts must then decide whether to allow the action of wind and wave to disperse the oil, or to use artificial dispersal methods. Spraying the slick with detergents allows the oil to mix more easily with the water. The oil-water mixture is then dispersed throughout the volume of the sea-water instead of lying wholly on the surface. However, this mixture of oil and water can seriously damage marine life as it sinks to the bottom of the ocean.

Nuclear pollution

Accidents at nuclear power stations and the atmospheric testing of atomic bombs cause radioactive gases to escape into the atmosphere. At present less than 1 per cent of the total radiation in contact with the general public comes from these sources. About 68 per cent of radiation exposure is due to natural radiation from granite rocks and cosmic rays. These natural sources have been around for millions of years and together with medical x-rays make up over 98 per cent of the public's total exposure to radioactivity.

Solid nuclear waste is extremely dangerous. Fortunately the amount of waste produced by a nuclear power station is small. The same amount of energy can lead to 1 tonne of nuclear waste or 100,000 tonnes of coal ash. Nevertheless the dangers are real because the waste retains its radioactivity for a very long time. The waste does decay with time but it can take the slowest form some 500 years to decay to the strength of natural background radiation.

Transport pollution

Modern transport has made many of our cities noisy, dirty and unattractive places to live in. Petrol fumes, poisonous carbon monoxide and lead from car exhausts pollute the air we breathe. In America strict laws now govern emissions from car exhausts. Some countries have been slow to follow America's example because anti-pollution measures can increase petrol consumption by up to 15 per cent.

Energy crisis

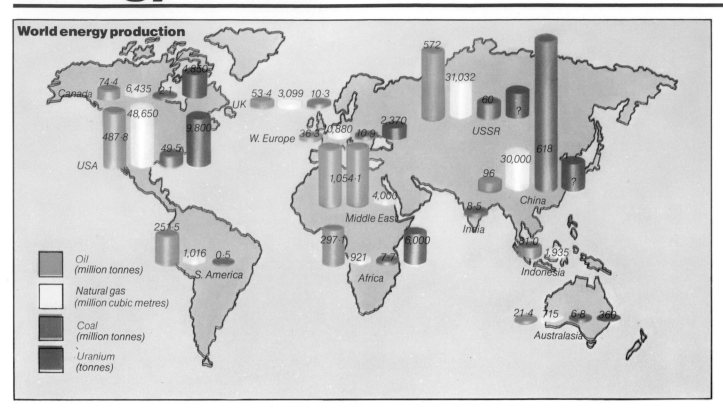

World energy production

Canada 74·4 6,435 2·1
4,850
USA 48,650
487·8 9,800
49·5
UK 53·4 3,099 10·3
W. Europe 36·3 10,880 10·9
2,370
572 31,032
USSR
60
?
618
30,000
96
China
?
Middle East 1,054·1
4,000
India 8·5
S. America 251·5
1,016 0·5
Africa 297·1
921 7·7 6,000
31·0
Indonesia 1,935
Australasia 21·4 715 6·8 360

Oil (million tonnes)
Natural gas (million cubic metres)
Coal (million tonnes)
Uranium (tonnes)

About 60 per cent of all the energy used in the world today comes from burning oil and natural gas. Despite massive exploration programmes, very few large oilfields have been found in recent years. This could well mean that most of the world's oil has already been discovered, and that, in the future, oil could run out faster than anticipated.

Trends
Today, the world is producing enough oil to meet its present needs. If only we could continue to use oil at its present rate, then world reserves could last for over 100 years. Unfortunately, world energy demand has been growing steadily over the past 50 years, and most experts believe that this trend will continue. No-one can say exactly how much energy will be needed in the future, but by the early 2000's demand for oil and gas will certainly exceed available supplies. This problem about our future energy supplies is often called 'The Energy Crisis'.

A great deal of the world's oil comes from a small number of Middle Eastern countries. Political events in this area such as the Yom Kippur war of 1973 and the unrest in Iran in 1979 seriously affected world oil supplies. Similar upheavals in the future could shorten the time we have to prepare for this coming crisis.

Solutions
The only solution to the problem lies in the development of both new and existing sources of energy. A wise country would use a mix of energy sources. But at the present time there is no technology capable of replacing oil, especially as a petrochemical feedstock. Traditional power stations take 10 years from planning to completion. New untried sources are therefore likely to take very much longer. Only by carefully conserving all our existing energy supplies can we 'buy time' to prepare for the future. In the early 21st century most of our energy will probably come from our plentiful supplies of coal.

Thermal nuclear power stations could supply a large part of our electricity needs, but eventually the world will run short of uranium. If the safety of fast breeder reactors was proved then this fuel problem would not arise for hundreds of years.

On the other hand, if nuclear power is abandoned for environmental or safety reasons, renewable sources will have to make up the deficit. Many countries still have great potential for hydro-electric power. Biofuels may satisfy the energy needs of a few countries where the climatic conditions are appropriate. Some tidal power stations may yet be built, but not enough to make a large impact on world energy supplies. The

Above: The world's current production of oil, natural gas, coal and uranium is here shown broken down by major region or country.

Below: The Middle Eastern countries form the majority of the members of OPEC. This organization wields an enormous influence over the rest of the world through the 'oil weapon'.

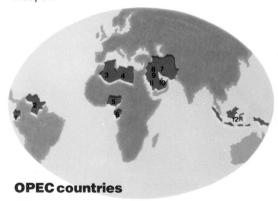

OPEC countries

1	Ecuador	**7**	Iran
2	Venezuela	**8**	Iraq
3	Algeria	**9**	Kuwait
4	Libya	**10**	United Arab Emirates
5	Nigeria	**11**	Saudi Arabia
6	Gabon	**12**	Indonesia

technology is not yet established for wind and wave power.

World reserves of poor-quality heavy oil, tar sands, and oil shales are enormous, and these doubtless will be more

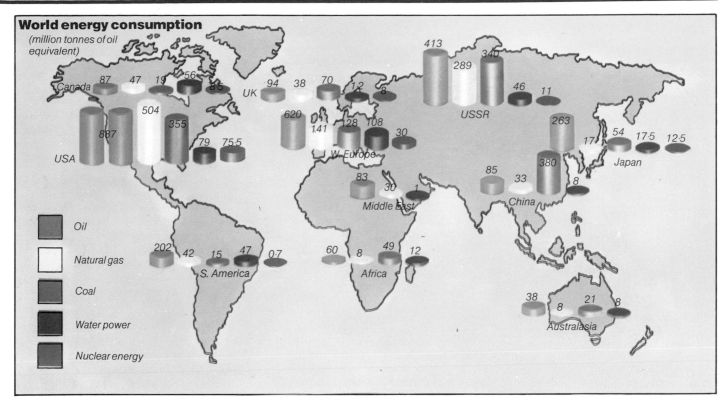

World energy consumption
(million tonnes of oil equivalent)

Canada 87 47 19 56 8·5
USA 887 504 355 79 75·5
UK 94 38 70 1·2 8
620 1·41 128 108 30
W. Europe
413 289 340 46 11
USSR
263 17 54 17·5 12·5
380 8 Japan
85 33
China
83 30 1
Middle East
202 42 15 47 0·7
S. America
60 8 49 12
Africa
38 8 21 8
Australasia

Legend:
- Oil
- Natural gas
- Coal
- Water power
- Nuclear energy

Above: This chart shows the world's current energy consumption levels broken down by major region or country. In comparison with the production chart opposite, several interesting points arise. Essentially, there is an imbalance because the major consumers are rarely major producers.

Right: Weapons of war use a great deal of energy. The superpowers may be willing to go to war to prevent the military from running short of fuel. This annual May Day parade in Moscow is where Russia shows off her military hardware.

fully exploited in the future. But if the nuclear option is taken up, then cars, buses and planes may run on hydrogen. If not, then oil derived from coal would be a possible alternative. Biofuels such as methane and alcohol may become important transport fuels.

Prospects

No-one can be sure whether these measures will be sufficient to cope with world demands, but it is likely that some countries will face the crisis sooner than others. There is a growing concern about the measures some of these countries may take to maintain their energy supplies. The unpredictability of the situation is mirrored in the world reaction to the Russian intervention in Afghanistan. Several countries would seem to be willing to go to war to safeguard their threatened oil supplies.

A-Z Glossary

Aerogenerator is the modern name for a windmill.

Alternative energy sources are those now being developed to replace the traditional fuels of coal, oil and gas. Solar, wind, wave and tidal energy sources are often described as alternative sources. The picture below shows the solar furnaces at Odeillo, France.

Anthracite is the hardest type of coal. It contains over 90 per cent carbon.

Arrester is a device inside industrial chimneys which prevents dirt and dust from polluting the atmosphere. Some arresters trap the dirt in a filter bag while others attract dust particles from the waste gases by means of an electrostatic field within the chimney.

Atomic number of an element is the number of protons in the nucleus of its atom. Each element has a different atomic number.

Atoms are the tiny 'building bricks' of all material. An atom has a central nucleus made up of even smaller particles called protons and neutrons. A number of electrons orbit the central nucleus.

Biofuels are fuels derived from plant material.

Biomass is organic material which can be converted into biofuel.

'Blow-out' is a dangerous escape of oil from a well head, caused by a sudden increase in oil pressure.

Carbohydrates are produced by plants from carbon dioxide and water as a result of photosynthesis. Sugars and starch are both carbohydrates and form the main energy source in the human diet.

Carbon is an element present in most substances from which we obtain energy. Fossil fuels and their by-products are all rich in carbon. Carbon compounds give up their energy in the form of heat by combustion (burning).

Cerenkov radiation occurs as a faint blue glow around the fuel elements of a reactor. It is caused by sub-atomic particles passing through a transparent medium at a speed greater than that of light in that medium.

Chain reaction is a process in which one change stimulates further changes of a similar type. When uranium atoms undergo nuclear fission, neutrons are emitted. These bring about fission in other uranium atoms so that a chain reaction occurs.

Chlorophyll is the chemical pigment which gives a plant its green colour. Without chlorophyll plants could not make use of the energy in sunlight so essential for photosynthesis.

Christmas tree is a series of valves mounted over the well head to control the flow of oil.

Coal occurs underground in layers or seams which sometimes outcrop at the surface. If this occurs then the coal can be quarried directly by opencast methods. Most coal is obtained by excavating shafts down to the seam. There are many kinds of coal. The more carbon coal contains, the higher its grade. In general the older the deposit, the higher is its rank and its efficiency as a fuel. The majority of our coal is bituminous (70-90 per cent carbon). Other forms are lignite or brown coal, anthracite, and peat.

Coolant is a fluid used to carry away heat from a hot surface.

Deuterium is an isotope of hydrogen essential to the fusion process. It is only available in small quantities but the potential energy of the deuterium available in one cubic kilometre of sea-water is equivalent to that stored in the world's total known oil reserves.

District heating systems distribute heat energy from a central source to a large number of houses. Most systems use underground hot water pipes to carry this energy.

Dynamo is a device which converts mechanical energy into electrical energy.

Efficiency. All energy convertors produce some unwanted forms of energy. The efficiency of an energy convertor is the percentage of input energy that is converted into useful forms.

Fast breeder reactor. Conventional thermal reactors use moderators to slow down the neutrons freed by the fission of the fuel nucleii. This increases their chances of being 'captured' by other fuel nucleii and so sustaining the chain reaction. Fast reactors use highly-enriched fuel (fuel which contains a large percentage of nucleii which can fission easily). A chain reaction can then be sustained without the need to slow down the fast neutrons. Breeder means that the reactor can produce more fuel than it uses.

Fossil fuels such as coal, oil and gas are derived from prehistoric plant material that has decomposed and been altered by heat and pressure over the years.

Geiger counter is an instrument for measuring the presence of radioactive materials. The small glass tube contains two electrodes. Radioactive particles break up the air molecules in the tube, releasing electrons. These electrons cause a measurable electric current to flow through the tube.

Geothermal power taps the huge resources of heat energy below the Earth's surface to generate electricity.

Heat exchanger is a long coiled tube through which a hot substance is made to flow. The coil acts as a heater, and is commonly used to transfer heat energy to water in a tank.

Horsepower is a measure of mechanical energy. If you could lift a 250 kilogram weight up from the ground to a height of 30 centimetres in one second, then you would have used up one horsepower of mechanical energy.

Hydrocarbons are substances formed by combining carbon and hydrogen. Oil is particularly rich in hydrocarbons.

Hydro-electric power is electricity generated by using the kinetic energy of water flowing down river valleys. A reservoir of water is created by placing a dam across the valley. Water pressure increases with depth so the higher the dam above the valley floor, the greater the pressure or 'head' of water available for the production of electricity.

Infra-red radiation is the invisible part of the Sun's spectrum otherwise known as radiant heat.

Insulators do not conduct an electric current. They are used in power cables to stop high-voltage currents leaking to earth and to prevent short circuits when two wires come into contact.

Internal combustion engine harnesses the combustion process (the burning of fuel to liberate energy) in the confined space of a cylinder.

Internal respiration is the reaction which takes place within living cells to convert the chemical energy stored in carbohydrates to other useful forms of energy.

Isotopes. The nucleus of an atom contains both protons and neutrons. Atoms of the same element all have the same number of protons. Isotopes are forms of the same element which contain different numbers of neutrons.

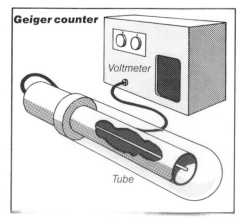

Geiger counter

Voltmeter

Tube

Joule is the international unit by which all forms of energy are measured.

Kinetic energy is the form of energy possessed by moving objects.

Lignite, or brown coal, is a soft coal and contains less than 70 per cent carbon.

Liquid petroleum gas is gas derived from oil and liquefied for easy storage. Butane and propane are the most common liquid gases.

Mass number is the number of nucleons in the nucleus of an atom.

Methane is a hydrocarbon gas occurring naturally as marsh gas. It is formed by the decay of vegetation in the absence of air. Sewage decomposition also produces methane which can be used commercially as a fuel. It may explode if mixed with air and is the cause of many mine explosions.

Moderator in a nuclear reactor is a substance into which the control rods are immersed to slow down the 'fast neutrons' and enable them to be captured by a uranium 235 nucleus. Graphite or water are used as moderators.

Natural gas is commonly used to describe gases with a large methane content found underground, often associated with oil deposits.

Nuclear fission is the reaction in which an atomic nucleus breaks up into two roughly equal parts.

Nuclear fusion is the reaction in which atomic nucleii join together or fuse.

Nucleus is the small central part of an atom which contains even smaller protons and neutrons.

Octane number is a rating for the fuel used in engines. The higher the octane number the higher the compression ratio of the fuel and air mixture that can be used.

Oil was formed in much the same way as coal. The essential difference is that whereas coal is formed from plant remains, oil comes from plants and tiny animals that once lived in water.

Oil refinery is a large industrial complex where crude oil is converted into finished products such as bitumen, diesel oil, petrol and bottled gas.

Oil wells consist of a surface structure called a derrick which supports a block and tackle that holds the drill pipe upright. The drill pipe is a hollow steel rod with a diamond-studded drill bit that cuts through solid rock. The rotating bit grinds the rock into powder which is brought to the surface by pumping a mixture of soft mud and water down the hollow drill pipe. The walls of the hole are lined with steel set in concrete to stop them caving in. When oil is struck the derrick is removed and the well is plugged with a complicated system of valves called a christmas tree.

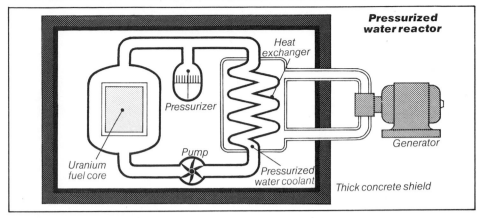

Pressurized water reactor

Heat exchanger

Pressurizer

Uranium fuel core

Pump

Pressurized water coolant

Generator

Thick concrete shield

OPEC is the Organization of Petroleum Exporting Countries. It is largely responsible for controlling world oil prices.

Paraffin is a hydrocarbon mixture obtained in the distillation of petroleum. It is used in lamps and domestic heaters.

Peat is a dark brown fibrous substance that has a high enough carbon content to make it a good fuel. The peat is cut and left to dry in the sun before being compressed into briquette form.

Photosynthesis is a reaction taking place in green plants which allows the energy of sunlight to be converted into potential chemical energy. The reaction involves the manufacture of carbohydrates from carbon dioxide and water. Only plants containing the green chemical chlorophyll allow the reaction to take place.

Power is the rate of doing work. The international unit of power is the watt. A one watt device converts one joule of energy from one energy form to another every second. Horse-power is also a unit of power: 1 hp = 746 watts.

Pressurized water reactor is a thermal nuclear reactor pioneered in the USA which uses pressurized water both as a coolant and a moderator. This reactor may form the basis of Britain's future nuclear energy programme.

Radioactivity is caused by the decay or disintegration of unstable atomic nucleii or naturally-occurring radioisotopes. This process can happen in a fraction of a second or take millions of years and is accompanied by the emission of *alpha-* or *beta-* particles or *gamma* rays from the nucleus. These particles or rays can be harmful to animal and plant life so precautions are taken whenever radioactive substances are used. Small doses of radiation can be beneficial for certain medical conditions.

Refuse-derived fuel is fuel manufactured from rubbish.

Renewable source is an energy source which will always be available to man. Solar, wind, waves, running water, and tides are thought of as 'the renewables'. Some people often add geothermal sources to the list.

Seismic survey is a technique which gives useful information about underground rock formations. Shock waves usually produced by an explosion travel at different speeds through different rock types, and the results are picked up by a series of detectors at the surface known as geophones. The time taken for the waves to reach the geophones provides the information about the underground rocks.

Solar cell is a device for converting light energy into electrical energy. Solar cells are made from semiconductors. The same material is used to manufacture transistors.

Tides are largely caused by the gravitational pull of the Moon, and to a lesser extent the Sun, on the waters of the Earth. The greatest variation in tides occur along coastlines. The highest tides occur in the Bay of Fundy, Canada.

Trap is an underground rock formation where oil and gas can be found. Common traps include salt domes, anticlines and faults.

U-value is a measure of the heat-conducting properties of a material. A good thermal insulator such as polystyrene foam, or fibreglass used in insulating a loft (*below*), has a very low 'U' value.

Ultra-violet radiation is the invisible part of the Sun's spectrum which is responsible for the skin getting suntanned. Intense ultra-violet radiation is extremely harmful to living organisms.

Uranium is a naturally-occurring radioactive element and is the major fuel in nuclear power stations.

Reference

The story of energy

The chronology below lists a few of the many milestones that have been passed in the last 200 years.

1769. James Watt patented the improved steam engine.

1831. Michael Faraday demonstrated the electric generator.

1859. Edwin Drake drilled the first commercial oil well.

1864. James Clerk-Maxwell predicted the existence of different kinds of electromagnetic radiation.

1896. Henri Becquerel discovered radioactivity.

1897. J. J. Thompson discovered the electron.

1905. Albert Einstein published his theory of relativity. The theory inter-related mass and energy according to the equation $E = mc^2$.

1911. Ernest Rutherford explained the existence of the nucleus.

1932. James Chadwick discovered the neutron.

1942. Enrico Fermi designed the first nuclear reactor.

1945. The first atomic bombs devastated Hiroshima and Nagaski, Japan.

1952. The hydrogen bomb is tested in the Pacific by the USA.

1956. The first atomic reactor to generate electricity became operational at Calder Hall, England.

The following scientists have made a great contribution to the history of energy.

Michael Faraday (1791-1867)

In August 1831, Michael Faraday, the brilliant English scientist, began a series of experiments which led to the development of the electricity generator. Faraday's device consisted of a copper disc which could rotate between the poles of a magnet. A device quite unlike the electricity generator which today produces most of the world's electricity.

Faraday's scientific genius was all the more remarkable because he was almost entirely self-taught. Born the son of an English blacksmith, Faraday's passion for science overcame his lack of scientific education. Today Michael Faraday is also remembered for his pioneering work in the development of the electric motor, his experiments on transformers and the formulation of the laws of electrolysis.

James Prescott Joule (1818-1898)

Such was Joule's interest in science that he is reported to have been seen measuring the temperature of the water in a waterfall while on honeymoon in Switzerland.

Joule did not earn his living as a scientist, but worked as a brewer in Manchester. In 1843 he invented a device which showed that a fixed amount of mechanical energy always produced the same quantity of heat. He did this by allowing a falling weight to turn paddle wheels in a tank of water. He then measured the water temperature before and after churning. Today one of Joule's original paddle wheels can be seen at the Science Museum in London. As a tribute to Joule's important contribution to the understanding of energy, the international unit for energy is now called the joule.

Antoine Henri Becquerel (1852-1908)

Becquerel was the French physicist credited with the discovery of radioactivity. Becquerel was interested in Röntgen's discovery of X-rays, and thought that fluorescent materials also gave off these strange rays. In 1896 he discovered by chance that uranium ore had darkened an unexposed photographic plate which had been left close by and thus established that uranium gives off radiation. This strange new phenomenon was later named radioactivity by another French scientist, Marie Curie.

Ernest Rutherford (1871-1937)

Brought up on a farm in New Zealand, Ernest Rutherford received his university education at Canterbury University in Christchurch. After graduating, Rutherford taught for a short time before taking up a position at the Cavendish Laboratory in Cambridge, England.

In 1899, following on the work of Becquerel, Rutherford identified *alpha* and *beta* radiation. He is, however, better known for his discovery in 1911 of the nucleus. Although the actual experimental work was carried out by a young student, Ernest Marsden, it was Rutherford's brilliant interpretation of the results which was of prime importance.

Albert Einstein (1879-1955)

In 1905, while working as a patent examiner in Berne, Switzerland, Albert Einstein published five papers which revolutionized three branches of physics. Perhaps the most famous scientific equation, $E = mc^2$, was contained in one of these papers. This equation states that energy can be converted into mass and vice versa, and that vast amounts of energy are locked up in matter. To date every experiment carried out has fitted Einstein's theory.

In later years Einstein moved to America where he became Professor of Physics at the Institute for Advanced Study at Princeton, New Jersey. He remained in the USA until his death in 1955.

Energy equivalents

One tonne of oil equals approximately 1.5 tonnes of coal, 5.3 tonnes of peat, 1,167 cubic metres of natural gas, or 12,600 kilowatt hours of electricity.

Books to read

Discovering Energy by Frank Frazer (Stonehenge Press, 1981)

Energy (Arco 1978)

Energy by Jim Jardine (Heinemann Editions, 1980)

Understanding Energy by Michael Overman (International Publications Service, 1975)

Machines and Energy by Eric Barker and W.F. Millard (Arco, 1972)

Fundamental Physical Forces by Raymond A. Wohlrabe (Lippincott, 1969)

Mining Coal by John Davey (Dufour Editions)

Coal: The Rock that Burns by Walter Harter (Elsevier-Nelson, 1979)

The Student Scientist Explores Energy and Fuels by Kaplan and Lebowitz (Rosen Press, 1981)

The Story of Oil by Roger Piper (Dufour Editions)

The Quest for Oil by W.G. Roberts (S.G. Phillips, 1977)

Oil by Roger Vielvoye (Viking Press, 1977)

Oil Rig by Neil Potter (Silver Burdett, 1978)

Oil by Neil Potter (Silver Burdett, 1980)

How Did We Find Out About Oil by Isaac Asimov (Walker and Company, 1980)

How Did We Find Out About Coal? by Isaac Asimov (Walker and Company, 1980)

How Did We Find Out About Solar Power by Isaac Asimov (Walker and Company, 1980)

Save that Energy by Robert Gardner (Julian Messner, 1981)

Saving Energy (National Geographic, 1981)

Feast or Famine? The Energy Future by Franklyn M. Branley (Harper and Row, 1980)

Solar Energy by John Hoke (Franklin Watts, 1978)

Energy abbreviations

ac/h	Air changes per hour
AGR	Advanced gas-cooled reactor
CHP	Combined heat and power
i-r	Infra-red
J	Joule
kWh	Kilowatt hour
LMFBR	Liquid metal fast breeder reactor
LPG	Liquified petroleum gas
mtce	Million tons of coal equivalent
mtoe	Million tons oil equivalent
m/s	Metres per second
OPEC	Organization of Petroleum Exporting Countries
PWR	Pressurized water reactor
rdf	Refuse-derived fuel
SI	Systéme internationale
SNG	Substitute natural gas
TAPS	Trans-Alaskan pipeline system
u-v	Ultra-violet
W	Watt

Pollution

The diagram on pages 40-41 depicts 27 ways in which the land, sea and air can be polluted. This is by no means comprehensive but shows that atmospheric pollution can be caused in 12 ways, that land pollution has at least 6 causes, and water is polluted by 9 sources.

Atmospheric pollution can be caused by the 'Space Age'. The rocket taking off jettisons both fuel and debris above the atmosphere whilst the exhaust gases remain in the atmosphere. Aircraft cause noise pollution, supersonic aircraft like Concorde create a shock wave 'boom.' The vapour trails behind aircraft are a mixture of unburned fuel, soot particles, and water. Pollutants from industrial chimneys in the picture are distributed throughout the atmosphere by winds and air currents. The build-up of carbon dioxide in the atmosphere as a result of this causes solar heat to be trapped within the atmosphere. Pesticide spraying by aircraft causes both land and atmospheric pollution. The chemicals can build up in animals and disrupt food chains. The cooling towers transfer waste heat to the atmosphere. Nuclear power stations could spring a leak and radioactive coolant might escape into the atmosphere. Pollutants from urban chimneys can cause eye and lung irritation. Waste products from refineries are burned off into the atmosphere.

Emissions from vehicle exhausts contain lead, unburned fuel, and carbon monoxide (poisonous gas). Most domestic fuels are inefficiently burned and steam or diesel boilers of tramp steamers can cause trails of gas and particles to be emitted.

The landscape is polluted by the coal mine and quarry in the picture. The slurry or excavated material is left to form unsightly tips. Electricity pylons and motorway hoardings are examples of visual pollution. Waste is often dumped rather than going to the expense of recycling. Modern litter unfortunately includes a high proportion of products like plastics which cannot be easily broken down. Motorways and airports occupy large areas of valuable agricultural land. Modern industrial estates pose waste-disposal problems on a massive scale.

Water is the easiest dustbin for man. Agricultural pesticides pollute streams, industrial effluents and sewage pollute rivers but because water is an efficient transport medium it all ends up in the coastal seas. These waters have the highest marine food productivity so the effects could be incalculable. Radioactive and corrosive wastes are dumped on the sea bed without a thought as to leakage. Oil tankers coming close to shore increase the risk of an accident. Oil slicks can be discharged into the sea accidently, on purpose, by oil rig blow-outs, or collisions.

Further information

You can find out a lot more about energy by writing to the following and asking them to send you free copies of their educational and promotional literature.

The National Energy Foundation
366 Madison Avenue
New York, New York 10017

The American Petroleum Institute
2101 L Street NW
Washington, DC 20037

The National Petroleum Council
1625 K Street NW, Suite 601
Washington, DC 20006

Edison Electric Institute
90 Park Avenue
New York, New York 10016

The American Gas Association
1515 Wilson Blvd.
Arlington, VA 22209

The National Coal Association
1130 17th Street NW
Washington, DC 20036

Exxon Corporation
Public Affairs Department
1251 Avenue of the Americas
New York, New York 10020

Mobil Corporation
150 East 42nd Street
New York, New York 10017

You may also want to write to the Public Relations Office of your local natural gas, electric utility, or municipal power company. These addresses would be available from your local library or in the telephone directory.

Acknowledgements

The statistics that form the basis of the two diagrams on pages 42-43 were taken from the *BP statistical review of the world oil industry 1978*.

Artists
John Davis, Keith Duran, Tony Gibbons, Elpin Lloyd-Jones, Clive Spong, and Craig Warwick by courtesy of Linden Artists; also Tom Macarthur, and John Marshall.

Photographs
Key: T (top); B (bottom)

Allsport: 18
British Petroleum Co Ltd: 37
Camera Press: 43
Daily Telegraph Colour Library: 15
Department of Energy: 32
Eurisol UK Ltd: 45
Richard Garratt: 12-13
Alan Hutchison Library: 20, 21, 25, 33
Lloyd's Register of Shipping/CMB SA: 28
Peter Loughran: 2-3
Richard McBride: 13, 35, 44
NASA: 17
Rex Features: 39
Bill Tingey: 34
UKAEA: 31T
Zefa Picture Library: front cover, 9, 10, 11, 14, 27, 31B, 38

Below: This diagram traces the pattern of world energy supplies by source over the period 1900-75 and goes on to project the future pattern up to the year 2050. It assumes a fairly low growth in energy demand per year and an optimistic forecast of future fuel supplies.

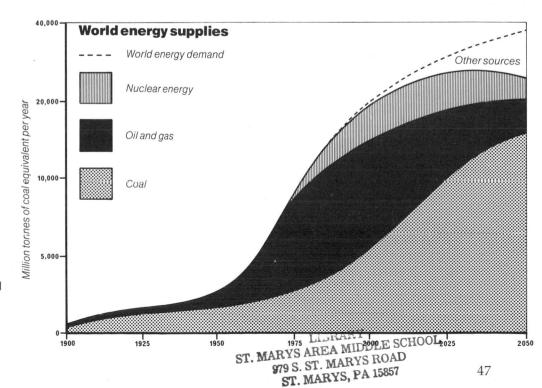

127549

Index

1 2 3 4 5 6 7 8 9 10—U—85 84 83 82